A PLUME BOOK

DISCOVER YOUR INNER ECONOMIST

TYLER COWEN is a professor of economics at George Mason University. He is a prominent blogger at marginalrevolution.com, the world's leading economics blog. He also writes regularly for the *New York Times*, and has written for *Forbes*, the *Wall Street Journal*, *Newsweek*, the *Washington Post*, the *Los Angeles Times*, and the *Wilson Quarterly*. You can find more about Tyler Cowen at his home page, www.gmu.edu/jbc/Tyler/.

"Stands apart from its predecessors by making its revelations not so much about the way the world works as about the way we ourselves work (and play)." —*The Economist*

"In a highly discursive style, Cowen rockets from topic to topic, covering everything from how to talk your spouse out of buying a warranty on a new purchase to the reason a Malaysian woman spent 32 days in a glass room filled with 6,000 scorpions. . . . Cowen ventures where few economists have gone before." —*New York Magazine*

"Tyler Cowen is a rare bird: an economist who's a wonderfully entertaining writer but also a deeply humane thinker. *Discover Your Inner Economist* will certainly change the way you think about an array of subjects, ranging from ethnic food to marriage to our never-ending quest for novelty. But even more important, it'll give you a sense of the real possibilities the world has to offer, and show you how thinking better can actually help you live better." —James Surowiecki, author of *The Wisdom of Crowds*

"Tyler Cowen is an economist, culture vulture, restaurant critic, and the best blogger in the world. All roles are on display in *Discover Your Inner Economist*. It's charming, smart, and very, very creative. And it will change your life in the best way: in small steps." —Tim Harford, author of *The Logic of Life*

"Part life coach, part scientist, and part 'cultural billionaire,' Cowen is a master at making interdisciplinary connections, many of which will have you immediately economizing your life, in a good way." —Playboy.com

DISCOVER YOUR
INNER ECONOMIST

Use Incentives to Fall in Love,
Survive Your Next Meeting,
and Motivate Your Dentist

TYLER COWEN

A PLUME BOOK

PLUME
Published by the Penguin Group
Penguin Group (USA) Inc., 375 Hudson Street, New York, New York 10014, U.S.A. •
Penguin Group (Canada), 90 Eglinton Avenue East, Suite 700, Toronto, Ontario, Canada
M4P 2Y3 (a division of Pearson Penguin Canada Inc.) • Penguin Books Ltd., 80 Strand,
London WC2R 0RL, England • Penguin Ireland, 25 St. Stephen's Green, Dublin 2, Ireland
(a division of Penguin Books Ltd.) • Penguin Group (Australia), 250 Camberwell Road,
Camberwell, Victoria 3124, Australia (a division of Pearson Australia Group Pty. Ltd.) •
Penguin Books India Pvt. Ltd., 11 Community Centre, Panchsheel Park, New Delhi – 110 017,
India • Penguin Group (NZ), 67 Apollo Drive, Rosedale, North Shore 0632, New Zealand
(a division of Pearson New Zealand Ltd.) • Penguin Books (South Africa) (Pty.) Ltd.,
24 Sturdee Avenue, Rosebank, Johannesburg 2196, South Africa

Penguin Books Ltd., Registered Offices: 80 Strand, London WC2R 0RL, England

Published by Plume, a member of Penguin Group (USA) Inc. Previously published in a
Dutton edition.

First Plume Printing, June 2008
10   9   8   7   6   5   4

Copyright © Tyler Cowen, 2007
All rights reserved

 REGISTERED TRADEMARK—MARCA REGISTRADA

The Library of Congress has catalogued the Dutton edition as follows:

Cowen, Tyler.
   Discover your inner economist : use incentives to fall in love, survive your next meeting,
and motivate your dentist / Tyler Cowen.
      p.   cm.
   Includes bibliographical references and index.
   ISBN 978-0-525-95025-7 (hc.)
   ISBN 978-0-452-28963-5 (pbk.)
   1. Economics—Psychological aspects.   2. Incentive (Psychology)   I. Title.
   HB74.P8C69   2007
   330.01'9—dc22   2007016161

Printed in the United States of America
Original hardcover design by Vicky Hartman

Contents

DISCOVER YOUR
INNER ECONOMIST

1

I Want a Banana; I Buy One

IS IT STILL possible to learn something new about falling in love? Or how to avoid boring office meetings? The answer is yes—the stuffy old science of economics actually can make for a better life. Economics offers an understanding of markets, the incentives that drive human behavior, and how humans exchange valuables. This book will show you how to use fundamental economic principles to get more of what you want.

In the simplest economic setting, buyers and sellers create markets to come together and trade. Indeed sometimes it seems like there are markets in everything. The ideas of trade, and gains from trade, permeate virtually every aspect of our lives. You want a banana; you buy one. You want someone to fix your car, shirt, or plumbing; you pay someone to do it. Just look in the local newspaper or on the supermarket notice board. You want access to all the information in the world? Call an Internet provider, buy a connection, and then Google to the right florist for Valentine's Day.

There are even more exotic markets. A mother once offered $500 on the Philadelphia Craigslist.org site to any girl who would step forward to take her (surely charming) son to the prom. You can buy virtual-reality games to play with, and against, your pets. A twenty-two-year-old atheist asks the religious to pay him to go to church; of course he promises to go with an open mind. He charges by the hour. You can pay to have a group of "artists" kidnap and then humiliate you. William Shatner of *Star Trek* fame sold his kidney stone on eBay for $25,000. In India it is possible to rent a crowd for your next public demonstration.

Markets can simplify our lives. Want a banana? Go to a market, say your local store, and buy a banana. It may help to recognize which supermarkets are the best, or when a banana is overripe, but otherwise the procedure is fairly straightforward. But for many other human desires, using money in a marketplace does not work very well, and sometimes it doesn't work at all. Getting what we want is not always so simple.

Say you feel low because you've just broken up with a boyfriend or girlfriend. Characters on television sitcoms often advise "retail therapy"; the claim is that he who thinks that money doesn't buy happiness doesn't know where to shop in the mall. This is exactly wrong. The Beatles were closer to the truth when they sang "Can't Buy Me Love."

Rather than knowing where to shop, it is more important to know *how* to shop, and also to know when *not* to shop. To do well in life, to really fall in love, for instance, I believe we must learn what can be obtained by exchange—monetary or otherwise—and what we cannot trade for. The central concept of economics is not money but rather incentives. Quite simply, an incentive is anything that motivates human behavior, or encourages an individual to make one decision rather than another. An incentive can be money, but it can also be a tip, a smile, or an act of praise. An incentive can be a promise of lifelong devotion. So yes, you can use incentives to fall in love, even if The Beatles were right that money doesn't work.

The fundamental economic insight, oddly enough, is that *not everything can be bought with money*. This seems so obvious to the ordinary person that most of us don't think about it. Our Inner Economist knows that money cannot buy love, respect, or peace of mind. Our bosses—and employees—know that a bonus won't solve every problem in the workplace. If we can't buy it with money, there is just no marketplace for that object of desire.

Given that we don't have markets in everything, we have to motivate other people, and motivate ourselves, to get where we want to be. Understanding and tackling this problem will fill this book. Using incentives, and using markets in the most effective ways, is far more difficult than simply going out and buying a banana.

Many of the limitations of markets are rooted in the imperfections of the human mind. Markets always interact with the complexities of human motivation, and when they are set up crudely or without much thought, they tend to misfire. Why don't we have more markets in self-improvement? No, I don't mean the self-help books we buy just to feel we are trying. I mean truly binding contracts, whereby we promise to lose weight, but if we don't we must pay money to a stranger. That's right, put up some money and hire someone to make you diet—it sounds simple enough. But no, that won't make you *want* to lose weight, and building up that desire is usually the only real long-term solution.

Observers frequently believe that economists advocate the total commercialization of everyday life. We economists are accused of viewing all human choices in terms of dollars and cents. Or we supposedly believe that markets are always good, or that markets can solve all problems. I do know a few economists who hold these views, but they do not follow from the essential principles of economics.

One of the most important lessons of economics is how to cope with scarcity. We cannot always pluck bananas from trees, or get the best health care, or buy everything in well-lit, air-conditioned shopping malls. Economics developed out of a recognition of the fact that many things worth having don't just fall into our laps in the course of our everyday lives. Even ordinary personal things like falling in love, surviving your next meeting, and motivating your dentist. The real purpose of economics is to get more of the good stuff in life.

Of course, economics is also about the national and global scale as reported in the evening news, stock prices, and world economic forums. Economists have long dreamed of making the whole world a better place. And yes, economic analyses do explain why the citizens of some countries are taking delightful vacations in Paris, while others are plowing field corn under a 100-degree sun. The founders of the science developed economics because they felt the world was full of injustices and squandered life opportunities. Economics, a cherished creation of the eighteenth-century Enlightenment, stems from the same belief in liberty and progress that influenced the birth of the American republic. The Founding Fathers believed in the power of human liberty, that is, a society based on the idea of free and responsible individuals. It is a profoundly important fact, which I will discuss further in the next chapter, that you can't understand how incentives work if you don't understand the importance of a respect for human liberty.

Economics, when it serves to boost "the wealth of nations," as Adam Smith called it, takes people from want and misery to health and plenitude. All that is true and important. But for this book we will start with our jobs, our choices, and our personal relationships as foundation stones for all subsequent decisions. "Saving the world" will have to wait until chapter nine.

To be sure, this is not the only book that applies economics to everyday life. My colleagues and friends David Friedman, author of *Hidden Order: The Economics of Everyday Life,* and Steven Landsburg, author of *Fair Play,* both promote economics as a tool of universal reasoning. They urge us to apply the ideas of incentives, markets,

and property rights to our families, our jobs, and our personal allocation of time. But I often disagree with their advice and fear that they,
for all of their brilliance, play into the caricature of the economist.
Their approach implies that ordinary life is more like buying a banana
than we usually think. "Just go out and use markets and incentives" is
their mantra. This is, at best, risky advice.

In my view the complexity and diversity of human motivations
ought to underlie the very foundations of economic reasoning. How
people assess their choices usually depends on social context, such
as what motivations we perceive in those around us and how we think
our peers will perceive us. If we want to make better decisions so we
get more of the good stuff in life, we must learn how to distinguish one
social context from another. If we offer an olive branch in negotiations,
will this be seen as magnanimity or collapse? If we dress casually for a
job interview, is this a sign of weakness or strength? We must figure
out how other people identify and distinguish different contexts, and
thus what they think they are doing and what they think we are doing.
We must understand human beliefs.

For that reason, applied economics is as much of an art as a science. Economists cannot solve all of our problems, but contemplating
the complexity of human motivation will help us make better decisions. We can learn when to just go buy something—like a banana—
and when a more roundabout approach is needed. We will look at
ordinary life using two primary tools: an understanding of the power
(and limits) of incentives and a recognition of the complexity and diversity of human beings.

• • •

MOST PEOPLE THINK economics is dull. Many academic economists build their reputations by specializing in one narrow area of
knowledge. A 1996 article in the *American Economic Review*—the
flagship journal of the profession—was titled: "Aggregation Without

Separability: A Generalized Composite Commodity Theorem." Who would read a book full of that? Economics is called the dismal science for a reason.

Like professionals in any field, economists are prone to hiding behind terminology and jargon. We economists have a particular weakness for qualifying our claims to the point of obfuscating them. Harry Truman once asked for a one-armed economist, so that he could not be told "on the other hand. . . ."

The world has come to expect unintelligibility from economists. Charles Sykes, in his book *ProfScam*, reports how an actor was hired to pose as an eminent economist and present a lecture on "game theory," one of the most abstruse branches of the science. The actor did not know any game theory, or any economics for that matter, but was able to bluff his way through with a seemingly formidable technical presentation. No one in the audience figured out the ruse. Afterward the evaluations praised the speaker for his clarity and intelligence.

In China, one Matthew Richardson was invited to give lectures on economics to a prestigious course at Beijing University. The previously invited economist had dropped out, and through a mixture of Chinese error and British deception, this Oxford University undergraduate managed to wrangle a substitute invitation. Yet the twenty-three-year-old Richardson was an engineering major and did not know any economics to speak of. When Richardson showed up he was paid £1,000 and put up in a hotel. He gave nine hours of lectures over the course of two days. The lectures were based on pages he had ripped out of a high school economics textbook.

On the second day of the course Richardson was running out of notes; he also suspected that the translator might be catching on to his ruse. During a coffee break he ran out of the room and did not return. The BBC described the Chinese as "furious." Apart from being walked out on, nobody likes to be duped.

Economics, if practiced properly, can for the most part overcome the pitfalls of inhumanity, verbosity, and undue obfuscation. Here are three principles for distinguishing good economics from bad.

1. **The Postcard Test**

   It should be possible to take a good economics argument and write it out on the back of a moderate-sized postcard. If an argument has too many steps, at least one of those steps is bound to be radically uncertain. Or, if there are too many steps, we won't know how all those different steps fit together to establish the argument's conclusion.

   When my Ph.D. students come to me with new ideas, I first say in my sternest voice, "Give me the postcard version." Those who know me well enter my office shouting: "I have the postcard!" Those who say it is necessary to read their entire forty-six page essay to grasp their central claim are told to go back to the drawing board.

2. **The Grandma Test**

   Most economic arguments ought to be intelligible to your grandmother. Grandma may not agree, but she should at least know what the economist is talking about. If Grandma *is* the economist, and speaks jargon herself, try one of your unruly cousins.

3. **The Aha Principle**

   The Aha Principle is an extension of the Grandma Test. If the basic concepts are presented well, economics should make sense. Good economists believe that we live our lives according to economic principles that anyone can understand. Perhaps we do not always understand what we are doing when we make decisions, but economic arguments and mechanisms should be recognizable. After all, the argument is about us. So if some clearly expressed economic observation is to the point, it ought to stimulate the "Aha" parts of our brains. That may sound a bit metaphysical, but the idea is that a clearly expressed economic observation should really matter to us personally. It should be a revelation.

How would you feel if you read a biography of your life and found that none of the events were familiar, not even upon reflection? You might start to think that something is wrong, and the same is true for the claims of economics. If some economic insight doesn't make sense to you, there is usually something wrong with it, not you. On the other hand, as we all know, moments of "Aha" can be so strong and so convincing that they can shape our lives for years to come.

When the "Aha!" goes off, that is our Inner Economist speaking. This book is about generating those Ahas!, and thus it is about discovering, liberating, and strengthening the Inner Economist.

· · ·

WE MAY THINK we know some good economic principles and try to live by them. But holding on to misguided ideas seems an inescapable aspect of good old human fallibility. Our theories of how the world works, whether they are explicit or implicit, lead us to make mistakes. Our views of the world, and even (especially!) our views of ourselves, are rife with fallacies that can be seen through the lens of good economics.

Your Inner Economist sees patterns that you might not be seeing at first glance. This book is about uncovering these hidden patterns in the world, and in our choices. Pattern recognition is one key to making better decisions. If it isn't helping us see more patterns, it isn't good economics.

The psychologist A. deGroot performed some fascinating experiments with pattern recognition in the context of chess. He arranged chess pieces on a board as they would occur in the normal course of a game. He allowed both chess masters and chess novices to observe the arrangement. The pieces were then swept away and the masters and novices were both asked to re-create the placement of the pieces. The masters performed significantly better than the novices. So far that is no surprise. But deGroot repeated the same experiment with pieces placed on the board randomly, in no particular order. When asked to re-create the observed patterns, the masters did no better than the novices. The masters were remembering the piece placements not by having flawless memories, but by recognizing familiar patterns and ordering them in a meaningful way. The masters, having a far larger collection of patterns to draw upon, remembered much better than did the novices. But this inventory of patterns was of no use to the masters when the pieces were scattered randomly. Other studies have found that chess masters do not have superior memories in other walks of life.

Being a great (human) chess player is not about searching through every possible combination. World-class players remain formidable when they play at very high speeds; one study indicated that up to 81 percent of the variance in chess skill can be explained by how grandmasters play with less than 5 percent of the normal time available. The key feature to becoming a chess grandmaster is the ability to acquire and keep about 30,000 to 50,000 different patterns or recognition chunks in one's cognitive capacity. This is part of the rationale behind Malcolm Gladwell's hypothesis in *Blink*, namely our ability to make rapid but accurate snap judgments in many walks of life. Often we recognize a relevant pattern from our embedded mental storehouse of possibilities, even if we are not aware of doing so.

The point of the chess analogy is that we can use economics to expand our repertoire of "recognition chunks" for seeing patterns in human behavior, including our own behavior and, of course, our mistakes.

Economics has many facets. Some economists focus on the statistical measurement of human behavior. Steven Levitt of *Freakonomics* fame made his name by studying statistics about unusual or under-explored walks of life, such as crime, real estate agents, and sumo wrestling. Other economists try to predict the next business cycle or tomorrow's stock prices. Yet others build ever more complicated mathematical models of human behavior, sometimes under the heading of "game theory." Economists in think tanks agitate for one public policy over another. At a simpler level, many textbooks teach basic terminology and how to manipulate graphs and symbols. This book will do none of those things.

Instead I will focus on using economics to hone our skills of pattern recognition—in other words, how to discover our Inner Economists. In most real-world settings, we don't have the time or inclination to "crunch the numbers," even in the unlikely event that all the data stood before us (do you know your dentist's income-tax return, as needed to calculate his optimal bonus for good work?). We have to make rapid decisions, yet we want to make the best decisions possible. Even if we have months to ponder, we often have no more information than the bare-bones facts we started with. Yet reality is not just a "buzzin', bloomin' confusion," to borrow a phrase from William James. There is indeed an order—sometimes a hidden order—to the social world.

We will see that there is much to be hopeful about. Small improvements in understanding can bring a *much* better use of incentives, leading to *much* better decisions and *much* better lives. Human imperfection is not the end of the story, but rather the beginning of a search for all kinds of riches.

2

How to Control the World, the Basics

MONEY MAY HAVE bought Judas's betrayal and the infamous local government of New York's Tammany Hall, but it often isn't the best motivator, whether in the family or at work. If you want to control more of what happens around you, you need to know how to balance the kinds of incentives you offer.

Economist Colin Camerer took a poll at the Davos World Economic Forum, which plays host to many of the world's business titans and idea gurus. When asked what makes people tick, the responding participants cited "recognition and respect" as the number-one motivating factor in the workplace. "Achievement and accomplishment" came in second.

But not so fast—we cannot dismiss money altogether. It is obvious that economies without good monetary rewards perform poorly. Utopian communes collapse because no one does the hard work. The state socialism of the former Soviet Union led to queues and privation, not solidarity. Rather than trying to make consumers happy, managers met the artificial targets of the central planners—by cheating and lying if necessary. Few people did wonderful work "for the good of the Father-land." More commonly, Soviet citizens worked to improve their social status and to receive the goodies usually reserved for members of the Communist bureaucracy. Marxist rhetoric to the contrary, it was not possible to do without monetary incentives. The Soviet Union simply had an inferior—and less fair—version of rewards and punishments. Dollars and cents matter.

Robert G. Swofford, Jr., a postal worker from Seminole County, Florida, won $60 million in a lotto drawing. He took more than a month to come forward and claim the prize. No, he was not planning the associated media events. He kept his mouth shut and divorced his wife, from whom he had separated three years earlier. The couple later reached a private settlement for sharing the funds; the ex-wife received $5.25 million and an extra $1 million for their eleven-year-old son, in return for agreeing not to seek more of her ex-husband's winnings.

(By the way, if you are interested in karmic justice, Swofford was later shot several times, by accident, by two police deputies investigating a crime. He survived, and he later had to make an additional monetary settlement to his ex-wife's sister, with whom he had earlier fathered a child.)

So how do we square these differing perspectives? How much *does* money matter? And when money isn't enough to motivate people, what should we do?

The classic management analysis suggests that we should not offer bonuses unless we have good measures of success. Don't pay the mechanic for finishing the job until the car starts. Hospitals are reluctant to give doctors bonuses for having a high success rate when performing heart surgery. Many doctors would be reluctant to take on the most difficult cases for fear of damaging their performance record.

The case against indiscriminate bonuses is made stronger by workers who think that bosses use bonuses to reward favorites. Such workers see bonuses as building a powerful coalition of unfair forces, rather than boosting workplace morale.

Yet bonuses remain a common form of compensation. A little economic analysis can offer a lot of conflicting insights. How can we know how to get the best results in a given circumstance? I offer three parables to help those on a quest to discover their Inner Economist: the Dirty Dishes Parable, the Car Salesman Parable, and the Parking Tickets Parable. These ever-so-slightly tragic tales illustrate guidelines for applying penalties and rewards. But to understand which parable applies and when, we'll have to wield the deft touch of our emerging Inner Economist.

• • •

1. The Dirty Dishes Parable

Most of us have noticed that our children or our roommates neglect their responsibilities. Laundry sits in the washing machine for days on end. Dirty dishes stack up in the sink, especially if the clean dishes in the dishwasher have not yet been unloaded. The longer the dishes sit there, the less likely that the problem will be solved. Dishes are most likely to be cleaned up right after the meal. Once the dishes become "a stale task," the would-be cleaner has failed to meet his or her responsibilities. At that point many people stop thinking of the dishes at all.

To understand the limits of dollars and cents, we can try an experiment. We can pick one of our children and *pay* her (or him) to do the dishes.

Contrary to a naive interpretation of economics, money—dare I call it "bribing your kid"?—usually does not solve the problem. In fact, research suggests that the sink probably will become dirtier or at best stay the same.

The failure of the bribe reflects the complexity of human motivation. People are motivated by external factors, such as money, and also by factors internal to their psyche, such as enjoyment, pride, or wanting to do a good job for its own sake. Sometimes payment causes external motivations to replace internal motivations. Yet for some tasks internal motivations are what get the job done. Payment can be counterproductive.

If you tell your daughter she is obliged to do the dishes, that story will stick in her mind. She may not always heed her duty, but she will feel some need to cooperate and meet expectations. Your child believes, "My efforts matter for the family. I am a contributor." Furthermore your daughter will respect you for believing that you are the leader of the family, who is due some amount of obedience in his or her own right.

When we pay our children, the tale changes. She says to herself, "Doing the dishes is a job for money," and she feels less obligation. The parent becomes a boss rather than an object of deserved loyalty. It is a market relationship. The daughter is no more obliged to do the dishes than she is to become a lawyer, or to buy a piece of bubblegum in the store. After all, markets are about choice, right? We can expect dirtier dishes, and we undermine the integrity of the family to some small degree.

A daughter receives little status from her peers if she earns $20 for doing the dishes. More likely the associated status of working for her parents is negative. Don't think she will brag to her friends about how she got the money. Having her own job—which is a signal of adulthood and independence—is cooler. Money from parents, which feels like an allowance for an immature dependent, will not boost the daughter's internal motivation to do the dishes. But a payment from a supermarket employer—the gruffer the better, if only to make her feel she is out in the real world—will get her to show up on time. The same daughter who won't do the dishes will fight to get time-and-a-half pay for working on Sundays.

When money doesn't work, sometimes the best way to achieve results is to praise the doer for her aptitude and talent in the job, whether or not this praise corresponds to the facts. For those reluctant to lie, think of this tactic as a stab at a self-fulfilling prophecy rather than as a deliberate untruth. It is not perfect, but it does appeal to the desire to do a good job.

One study compared two methods for cleaning up a school. Authorities could a) lecture students that they should be neat and tidy, or b) compliment them for being neat and tidy. The lecturing had no effect, but the praise increased litter collection by a factor of three. The students saw a gain from identifying as clean and conscientious people; if anything, scolding usually makes such a self-image more difficult to adopt.

Laboratory research confirms that payment does not always lead to a better job done. Economists and psychologists put subjects into artificial settings and ask them to perform tasks, ranging from guessing the number of beans in a jar to performing household chores to solving a crossword puzzle. Often the subjects do just as well, or sometimes even better, when nothing is on the line. The dishes example is taken from my own home, but that episode is typical. The basic result has been observed and replicated for many tasks.

Sometimes the problem runs deeper; human beings are outraged by the idea of trading everything in markets. I read an advice column letter from a woman whose husband promised to "pay her by the pound" to lose weight. I'm guessing this marriage is not a happy one. I'm also guessing that she won't lose much weight or feel very good about this offer.

The very act of trading contradicts some of our most cherished values. Buying sex is relatively easy. Buying a particular kind of sex—say with love and passionate kissing—can be impossible.

That said, we still need to figure out when money will make a big difference.

2. The Car Salesman Parable

It is the simplest of the three stories. If you don't pay people, they won't sell cars.

Car salesmen typically receive bonuses from the number of cars they sell, and of course their bonuses are a percentage of the price they get. That's why they bargain so hard with us. Hardly anyone sells cars for fun.

On the brighter side, the incentives do mean that many cars get sold. While the salesman tries to get as high a price as possible, a salesman who abuses customers will lose business.

The car salesman parable is the simplest of our three stories, and it lies at the core of standard economic reasoning. The trick is to know when it does not apply.

3. The Parking Tickets Parable

This one shows that people often respond to the same incentives in very different ways.

Until 2002, United Nations diplomats enjoyed legal immunity for any parking tickets they incurred while on their missions to the United States. They could park wherever they wanted, including in front of fire hydrants, and ignore any legal penalties. Not surprisingly, many diplomats took advantage of this privilege. Between November 1997 and the end of 2002 in New York City, U.N. diplomats incurred more than 150,000 parking violations.

By far the most common violation was to park in a "No Standing—Loading Zone" area. Parking in front of fire hydrants was 7 percent of the total.

The distribution of these violations across countries was far from even. The thirty-one U.N. diplomats from Norway and Sweden had no unpaid parking tickets over this period of time. Diplomats from Canada, Ireland, the Netherlands, the United Kingdom, and Japan also had no unpaid parking tickets.

In contrast, Kuwaiti diplomats incurred more than 246 unpaid parking violations per diplomat. Egyptian diplomats were a distant second with a mere unpaid 139.6 violations per diplomat. The next eight worst violators, in order, were: Chad, Sudan, Bulgaria, Mozambique, Albania, Angola, Senegal, and Pakistan.

I do not believe that these countries have lots of color-blind diplomats who can't see yellow lines. Instead, most of these diplomats just don't have a huge amount of respect for the law. Many of them are downright corrupt, or were corrupt back in their home countries.

The point is this: the diplomats from Sweden and Kuwait faced the same immediate incentives when deciding to park and whether or not to pay a ticket. Yet the results were very different.

Why might this be? Let us step back and consider some context.

It is not easy to get a posh New York diplomatic assignment in lieu of a civil-service post in the glamorous N'Djamena, the capital of Chad. Consider this travel report from a few years back: "Chad's capital is slowly regaining its prewar reputation as one of Central Africa's liveliest cities. Bullet holes in buildings serve as a reminder of troubled times, but the atmosphere here is increasingly upbeat."

But oops, here is a *Washington Post* report from only a few years later: "Heavy shelling and machine-gun fire echoed through the capital of Chad on Thursday as rebels based in the Darfur region of western Sudan marched into the city and battled army troops, according to witnesses and news reports. State television broadcast images of bloody bodies of rebels, some still wrenching, piled on the steps of the National Assembly in N'Djamena, the capital. Witnesses reported seeing bodies in other areas of the city, news services said, and residents could be seen fleeing as helicopters hovered above."

Chad is clearly not one of the most stable countries. In such countries the culture of meritocracy is rare. The poorer the country, the more likely that their diplomats have received special treatment all of their lives, and they expect those privileges to continue. Corruption breeds subsequent irresponsibility. In fact, *the higher a country ranks on indexes of domestic corruption, the higher the number of unpaid New York City parking tickets reaped by its U.N. diplomats.*

This brings us to a key point for applying rewards and penalties: incentives matter through the medium of how a person perceives what is at stake in the choice. It is not just getting the mix of incentives right, you also have to know something of the values or cultures of the people you are dealing with.

In our particular example, Swedes are more likely to regard governments—whether their own or the governments of others—as morally legitimate. In turn they are more likely to obey laws, even in the absence of any immediately selfish motivation. Swedes also, on average, take greater care to cultivate their reputations as law-abiding citizens, if only for the sake of their future careers. Sometimes another diplomat is in the car, so not all of those parking violations are secrets.

Diplomats from Kuwait or Egypt or Chad are more likely to have made a living through corruption, special family connections, and flouting the law. They view a fire hydrant as a nuisance, not as a public good for the local community.

It isn't even just a matter of civil values. People express likes and dislikes indirectly. The parking ticket numbers also show that if a country has a favorable opinion of the United States, its diplomats are less likely to have large numbers of unpaid tickets. A Pew public opinion survey from 2002 indicated that the United States was most popular with the citizens of Honduras, Venezuela, Ghana, Philippines, and Nigeria. These countries did better on the parking-ticket index than would have been expected from their other characteristics. From the same survey, the countries viewing the U.S. least favorably were Egypt, Pakistan, Jordan, Turkey, and Lebanon. Egypt and Pakistan were both among the top-ten worst parking-ticket offenders. In other words, diplomats are more willing to behave irresponsibly when they have contempt for the country they live in.

The number of unpaid parking tickets goes up considerably as diplomats spend more time in New York City. Perhaps they learn the reality of diplomatic immunity. Or perhaps they learn there are few legitimate parking spots to be had in midtown Manhattan. In any case, the diplomats perceive the parking-ticket game differently. And the change in perception is greatest for those diplomats from high-corruption countries. With a little bit of time they learn which local laws must be respected (e.g., don't offer money to a cop) and which can be trampled.

Controlling people requires an understanding of the social context of the person we are trying to control with rewards and penalties. Does he or she see cooperation or "defection" as the default option chosen by her peers?

It is oversimplifying to claim that some societies are "simply more cooperative" than others. For instance, in Kuwait there is a tradition of extreme hospitality to visiting strangers; in Bedouin culture it has long been obligatory to help people lost in the desert, even if the aid involves considerable risk and expense. That is one kind of cooperativeness. The wealthier, safer, and more individualistic Sweden is kind to strangers in other ways, such as taking in immigrants, but they are more likely to view their responsibilities in terms of national government policy rather than tribal or clan relations.

No one is cooperative all the time. When what many Americans view as uncooperative behavior is framed as socially acceptable in Scandinavia, Scandinavians will flout duties, laws, and proper procedures.

Anyone who walks around Sweden or Norway will notice an especially tall, vital, and indeed healthy population. Scandinavian rates of longevity are among the highest in the world. Yet a recent study showed that about 25 percent of Norway's workers are absent from work on an average day. Usually they are "sick," they are "undergoing rehabilitation," or they are on long-term disability. The rate of absenteeism is especially high for government employees, who constitute about half the workforce. The otherwise cooperative Scandinavians think nothing of deciding to just stay at home. In Norway chronic absenteeism encounters few penalties. The first year of sick leave often meets with full pay for a year and 60 percent pay the second year. If an employee is fired, unemployment benefits are long and generous. Long-term disability leave is up 20 percent since 1990, yet overall, Norwegians are becoming healthier, not sicker.

Vacation time runs about five weeks for most people; Norway has eleven national paid holidays, and of course there are weekends. From these sources alone, Norwegians take off nearly half the calendar year, or about 170 days. Sickness, disability, and rehabilitation account for many extra free days.

The Norwegians are simply less keen on working and they are used to the idea that they do not have to work and should not have to work. They do not tend to think this belief makes them uncooperative. Norway is a wealthy society, and like most of contemporary Western Europe it glorifies leisure, not economic growth. Bravo for them, some of us might feel. Is not leisure time one of the greatest pleasures? But that is precisely the point. The Norwegians—and some of us—find this behavior entirely acceptable. But the ordinary resident of Chad, who works seven days a week, even when debilitated with malaria or dysentery, might find it unbelievable or horrifying.

Psychologists write about the "Fundamental Attribution Error," or "correspondence bias," as it is sometimes called. The error is to assume that a single instance of individual behavior represents a deeply rooted personality trait. Instead, the behavior is often the result of situational influences. For instance, if someone cuts ahead of us in line, we tend to assume the interloper is a bad person. But there is a good chance the cutter simply did not notice those ahead of him, perhaps because of stress.

Researchers offer numerous explanations for our tendency to typecast, but I find one factor to be especially common. We assume that other people frame choices the same way we do. For the other person, "what is at stake" is often very different from what we think is at stake. The Kuwaiti diplomats, in their own eyes, are not always "cynically taking advantage of the United States for their own personal parking gain." Sometimes they are engaging in "ordinary discretionary disregard for poorly thought out, unnecessary, and ill-suited laws."

Most of us have driven 40 miles per hour, or perhaps even 50 miles per hour, in a 25-mile-per-hour zone. Where I live, in northern Virginia, 35 is the average speed in a 25-mile-per-hour zone. We rationalize our disregard for the law by noting that many others do the same and that it is otherwise impossible to get around. But we don't usually drive that fast on our own street, especially if we have small children. We are not as different from the Kuwaiti diplomats as we like to think.

By the way, this parable shows why shareholders do not hire economists to run the world's largest and most profitable corporations. Economists have wonderful theories, but the trick is to know which particular theory applies when. Interpreting and understanding a person's beliefs is as much art as science.

In the final act of the parking tickets story, American public opinion led to a backlash against this behavior. The United Nations has long been an object of skepticism in the United States, and foreign diplomats are even less popular. New York City officials grew frustrated and Congress decided to act. The 2002 Clinton-Schumer Amendment gave New York City the right to tow the vehicles of diplomats with unpaid parking tickets. Furthermore delinquent fines would be subtracted, by Congress, from a country's foreign-aid allotment.

The number of diplomatic parking tickets dropped immediately by more than 90 percent. But the list of countries that accumulated the most and least number of unpaid tickets hardly changed.

· · ·

SO WHEN DOES each parable apply? When it comes to the use of monetary rewards and penalties, we cannot expect a single factor—the amount of money on offer, a person's commitment, or a person's understanding of others' expectations—to determine the right course of action. We must observe a cluster of related factors and then balance them out. The Car Salesman Parable is most relevant for motivating people when a combination of the following conditions holds:

1. Offer monetary rewards when performance at a task is highly responsive to extra effort.

   Clerical work requires attentiveness. Filing papers in the right order is tedious, but it is within reach of most of us. We need only try to get it right. Pay us more for a good result and we will try harder. This has been confirmed by laboratory experimentation.

Prizes and rewards also boost simple memory and recall skills, again provided the tasks are within the reach of most people. Tasks involving the careful matching of information, such as accounting work, call for rewards and bonuses as well. Prizes also motivate individuals to spot typographical errors. For the reasonably literate this task is largely a matter of vigilance.

Prizes and payments also induce individuals to endure more pain. One group of female subjects was asked to hold their hands in very cold ice water—about 32 to 35 degrees Fahrenheit—for four to eight minutes. Each woman received $2 for lasting four minutes and an additional $1 for each extra minute above four.

The paid subjects held their hands in the cold water for much longer than did the unpaid subjects; the difference was an average of 307 seconds versus only 110 seconds. This was a bigger difference than what participants had forecast prior to the start of the experiment—namely, averages of 355 seconds for the paid group versus 262 seconds for the unpaid group. In other words, the unpaid people lost their tolerance for enduring the discomfort more quickly than they had expected. Sometimes money matters more than we like to think it will.

But some activities are so easy and so transparent that a bigger prize doesn't help. For instance, when individuals bargain over the disposition of a dollar they strike about as good a deal as when they bargain over $100. There simply isn't much scope to try harder, and so the bigger stakes have no impact.

A young woman doing the dishes is a matter of effort, and so it might appear to fit this general category. Indeed it does apply when a restaurant hires a teenager to work in the kitchen. But

#1 does not usually apply to daughters, or to people who have passions, either positive or negative, about the task at hand.

2. Offer monetary rewards when intrinsic motivation is weak.

My wife spends some of her time tidying up the living room for the family. I would be crazy to start paying her for that. She already has the intrinsic motivation to do the job, and she earns a good living as a lawyer. She doesn't need money to support her cleaning habit. Dare I say she is passionately devoted to making a good home, so this is a strong intrinsic motivation? Conversely, I enjoy doing the family cooking (Mexican, Indian, and Chinese foods are my passion), and I do a better job by taking pride in my performance than by expecting payment.

Roland Fryer, an economist at Harvard, decided to conduct an experiment and pay students for better grades. A new pilot program will reward schoolchildren if they do well on reading and math exams throughout the school year. A score of 80, for instance, would receive a $20 bonus, with further payments for later improvements. Fryer remarked to a reporter: "There are people who are worried about giving kids extra incentives for something that they should intrinsically be able to do . . . I understand that, but there is a huge achievement gap in this country, and we have to be proactive."

Indeed there have been experiments with paying for grades. A school near Detroit, in the Birmingham school district, started paying third-graders "Beverly Bucks" for doing well on homework and tests. A spelling test is worth $2. Their "paycheck" was denominated in terms of dollars but it was good only in the school store. The children also paid taxes on the hallways and on the playgrounds. They could forfeit money, too. "If I accidentally hit somebody, I have to lose $4 or $5," said Shane Holmes, eight, who appeared to find a loss that size horrifying.

Fryer has yet to finish this experiment, but I have a prediction: this method will work best in bad schools, where children otherwise see no reason to do their homework or pay attention in class.

There is in fact a long history of paying students for good grades. It was tried as early as 1820, in the New York City school system, by the Society for Progressive Education. The system was abandoned by the 1830s, on the grounds that it encouraged a "mercenary spirit" rather than learning.

3. Pay monetary rewards when receiving money for a task produces social approval.

Actors know they "have made it" if they are paid $20 million per movie. They feel good about the money, not ashamed of it. That strengthens rather than displaces internal motivations to work hard and to work smart.

Hedge-fund managers receive ego boosts from their millions. They are driven individuals, obsessed with both money and status. Again, the two rewards work in the same direction.

For an intellectual eighteen-year-old girl, a job at Borders is both fun and cool. The manager can pay her to reshelve the books, even if her father can't pay her to do the dishes.

Given that bonuses appear counterproductive in so many experiments, many social psychologists have wondered whether a modern economy should significantly limit the use of cash payments. This fantasy view is a bunch of academics taking their own underpaid lives too seriously. Just because many professors improve their classes without any expectation of payment in return, it does not mean that we can run businesses on the same basis. Cash payments in the lab often backfire, just as they can backfire at home or in the workplace, because they are often applied poorly. A lab is a useful place to see what might happen, but it cannot tell us what, in the real world, *will* happen or *should* happen. The people who run the lab are not the same people who run businesses, nor can they create the same status rewards for an accomplishment. Businesses are masters of finding—and indeed creating—situations where cash payments and the drive for status work together to get people to perform.

The real question is when cash rewards work and when they do not. If factors #1, #2, and #3 (as listed above) are in place, we are likely facing a Car Salesman scenario. In other words, we should use money to motivate when effort matters, there is little intrinsic desire to do the job, and money boosts the recipient's social status. The absence of those same factors suggests a Dirty Dishes scenario.

I offer a couple of further qualifiers for using monetary rewards and penalties. For instance, we should be wary of offering rewards and penalties for individuals who are bringing faulty premises to bear on the problem, or individuals who overreact to feedback. I have no clue how to hit a golf ball down the course and into the hole. Paying me $1,000 for coming in under par would probably just intensify my application of bad habits. Sometimes trying harder makes everything worse.

In one study two groups of subjects were given some information about twenty students and asked to predict which of those students "won honors." The subjects also were given a formula for making the prediction and told it is very difficult to beat the formula. One group of subjects was asked to make predictions, but that group knew it would win nothing for getting it right. Most of that group stuck to the formula and had a success rate of 66 percent. The second group of subjects was offered money for correct picks. They were more likely to abandon the formula—they were "trying too hard"—and they had a success rate of only 63 percent.

Higher rewards might, in the long run, stimulate my interest in lessons and the arduous process of acquiring real golf skill. But in the short run, and often even in the medium run, the rewards will intensify basic, ingrained mistakes. When our judgment is messed up in the first place, and a great deal is on the line, we feel we need to do "everything possible." This compulsion is not always healthy for the final quality of performance.

Most petty criminals respond to immediate incentives for cash but they worry less about longer-term incarceration or failing life prospects. Richard T. Wright and Scott Decker, in their fascinating book *Burglars on the Job,* documented this short-term bias. They interviewed 102 petty burglars to find out what motivates their crimes.

The criminals almost always perceived themselves to be in a situation of crisis. They required a steady fix of immediately pleasurable experiences—usually women and drugs—and they acted to secure those experiences. In the absence of those fixes, the criminals felt anxieties. The requirement, as perceived by the criminals, was to eliminate the source of anxiety as quickly as possible. If the criminals didn't have enough money in pocket, as was often the case, they would organize a break-in. Honest day-labor did not relieve their anxieties within a sufficiently short period of time. Furthermore, legitimate work usually required subservience to a boss, which was about the worst possible fate for many of these people.

Getting petty criminals to think more about the future would do more than stiffer punishments to reduce these criminal acts. Often the criminals refused to engage in advance planning or calculate their risk. In objective terms few if any of these people were on the verge of starvation or extreme poverty. Criminals were driven by incentives—arguably too driven—but they looked at the immediate rewards and ignored the longer-term costs.

4. High rewards tend to make individuals "choke."

Oh, how we are afraid of making mistakes. Trying at a task, and running the risk of failure, brings stress or feelings of low self-esteem. I see these problems frequently in my role as dissertation advisor at the university. Many students are afraid they cannot write as well as they are supposed to. When more is at stake, they freeze up and make bigger errors. Some students abandon the dissertation altogether, simply because they feel overwhelmed by its importance. These people—who are highly intelligent—do better when the stakes are lower.

Let us say I were to walk to the free-throw line in basketball and try to make a basket in one attempt. I am a weak amateur in basketball and I am, to say the least, unaccustomed to the pressure of championship situations. I've never been asked to take the winning shot in a pickup game (outside of one-on-one, that is), much less in a professional setting. What kind of reward or penalty will maximize the chance that I hit the basket?

I suspect the optimal prize for the basket is about $100. That is just enough to grab my attention and induce my full concentration. $50 might suffice. If an evil tyrant, or perhaps a terrorist, threatened to chop off my head if I failed to make the basket, I am not sure I would respond well. I doubt if my chance of making the basket would go up. I don't want to have *too much* at stake. Having a large crowd watch me would make it only tougher.

In the Orson Scott Card famous science-fiction novel *Ender's Game*, an entire intergalactic war is fought using children who play war "games" on computer screens. The children are told it is an important competitive game, and they think it is a game. They have no idea that the very future of human civilization is at stake, or that a single shot will kill many real creatures in very real starships.

Stressed people tend to conform more to social opinion. They feel out of control and so they look to groupthink and the security blanket of other people's approval. What better "out" is there than to do what others tell us? If a mistake is then made, it wasn't really our fault. What is the implication? Don't stress those people whose judgment is critical to the success of a project.

This brings me to my second qualifying point about using monetary rewards to control people, and it cuts to the heart of the whole question. We must be wary of monetary incentives for people who feel they have lost control. Poorly applied incentives can exacerbate this feeling of helplessness and cause those people to behave destructively or to rebel just for the sake of rebellion. In other words, the application of punishments and rewards can make us feel like slaves. The result is often a poor performance. *Everyone needs to feel that he is in control of something.*

3

How to Control the World, Knowing When to Stop

LET'S CONSIDER THIS need for control in more detail.

We all know that exercise is good for our health, yet many people spend too much time on the couch. At least on the surface, an economist might appear to have an answer to this problem. We can set up or call upon markets to force ourselves to exercise.

We can "post a bond" with a friend, spouse, exercise partner, or someone we won't, or can't, lie to. Write out the check in advance. The agreement is simple. We lose the money if we don't exercise according to a prearranged plan with well-defined quantitative goals. Thirty push-ups a night, plus a gym visit every other day. If need be, I will serve as monitor and cash your check when it comes in the mail. I will ask for time-stamped photos.

Or the gym could play the role of enforcer. The gym would collect a bigger upfront fee, and *they pay us* each time we show up and complete an exercise program under their supervision. Who is better at monitoring compliance than on-the-spot professionals?

Yet such arrangements may scare us off from exercise altogether. We enjoy exercise, but not if we feel trapped by the obligation. As with the Dirty Dishes Parable, too many external incentives can diminish internal motivations. If exercise becomes a regular arena for money loss and humiliation, sooner or later we will avoid the exercise idea altogether. We will stop making these contracts.

Yes we want to exercise more, but we also want to feel in control. That is a fundamental human urge. If our exercise program makes us feel like slaves—even through *self*-imposed constraints—that program will probably fail.

We hear blather about "life being a process" that we can control. This is in some sense true, but it is less well-recognized that our concern with process is the root of many a personal failure. We do not obey when we ought to. How many of us would write to advice columnists—I mean the smart and insightful ones—if we knew we had to abide by the answer we received? We care too much about being in control of the process and not enough about getting the right outcome.

So, rewards and penalties often fail when individuals feel a resulting loss of control. When we do apply incentives, we should frame them with respect and at least the appearance of consultation. Get the rewards and penalties out of people's faces, unless of course those rewards bring social status. Otherwise, the more prominent the reward, the more likely it is to reduce intrinsic motivation.

This feeling of needing to be in control is not something we can do much about. The quest for control springs from deep psychological and biological urges. That is one reason why sensory-deprivation chambers are such an effective form of torture; they rob the victims of any feeling of control. It also explains why working on our own projects can be so satisfying, at least if they have some chance of success, or if we can fool ourselves into thinking they do.

The need for control is yet another reason why a daughter might not wash the family dishes for money. She fears a world where she becomes a puppet, at the continual beck and call of parental dollars. This is a major drawback of rewards and penalties. We use them to influence the behavior of other people. And this is precisely what makes those people feel a lack of control and a lack of freedom. Many people rebel against those feelings, or against the sources of those feelings, and that is why incentives can be so ineffective or perhaps even counterproductive.

. . .

THE IMPORTANCE OF feeling in control offers some further clues for improving the world, and improving ourselves. Trying to control other people can be disastrous. Sometimes it is simply necessary to stop and move on.

Let's return to the Parking Tickets Parable. That story shows just how much the kind of person—and the degree of that person's cooperativeness—can matter. In other words, what often matters is not controlling other people but rather finding like-minded others, or persuading others to understand a situation as you do.

The obvious business question is when we should pay for quality coworkers.

There is an old business maxim: "Pay to get talent and to keep it." That is a cliché, but we now get a better sense of when "having the best people" is worth the cost. When rewards and penalties will motivate, especially for simple tasks, the quality of the person matters less. Hire a drudge and pay him a bonus to file those papers.

We should pay more for talent when bonuses and intrinsic motivation will work together for very high levels of effort and achievement. In these cases social status reinforces rather than displaces monetary rewards. The drive to perform really matters. These are the high salaries, and also the bonuses, for top lawyers, investment bankers, and athletes. When they try harder, the best performers know what they are doing; it is not like me with my feeble golf swing.

We also should pay more for talent when the task is socially important but when end-of-the-year performance bonuses are weak or nonexistent. Institutions often rely on intrinsic motivation to get the job done, and we need to make sure we hire people with the right motivations. More concretely, we should pay more for schoolteachers, and yes, that includes me.

Sometimes it is not a question of paying more but rather reshaping the environment of surrounding peers. In 1990, H. Wesley Perkins, a professor at Hobart and William Smith Colleges, discovered that most students think they drink less than the average student. In fact they feel deficient and cowardly. Students feel pressure to drink more to be like the others. But of course not everyone can be below the average or for that matter above the average. These feelings are largely an illusion. We so often assume that others are going out more than we are or having more fun than we are. In reality we are more typical than we like to think.

When the true drinking numbers are publicized, students discover that few of their peers have more than five drinks at a party. The peer pressure to binge is reduced. The California state university system applied this public relations approach with success. Rather than telling students to "Just say no," it is more effective to say, "Just be like most everybody else."

Although I am an optimist at heart, I know that many incentive problems are for the most part insoluble. But we still might make a smidgen of progress. In the limiting case, sometimes we simply need to know when to give up. I have never had much luck trying to induce late people to be punctual. Usually I end up either tolerating their lateness or ending the relationship.

In Ecuador businesses and civic groups have led a recent national campaign to make people more punctual. Ecuadorians are famous for being late; a dinner party scheduled for 8 P.M. might not start until 10:30. To arrive at 9 P.M. would shock the hostess and would be considered inappropriate. This arrangement might be okay for socializing, but it is disastrous for business. According to one estimate, habitual lateness in Ecuador costs 4.3 percent of national income.

But now many businesses and government agencies have signed pledges to be prompt. They have promised to close meetings to late-comers. Two-sided signs have been printed. One side proclaims, "Come in: You're on time"; the other side says, "Do not enter: The meeting began on time." A local newspaper decided to publish regular lists of public officials who show up to events late.

One Ecuadorian poster read as follows:

Symptoms: Rarely meets obligations on time, wastes people's time, leaves things to the last minute, no respect for others

Treatment: Inject yourself each morning with a dose of responsibility, respect and discipline. Recommendation: Plan, organize activities and repair your watches.

The campaign has yet to succeed.

Many people have deeply seated emotional reasons for being late. Being early or on time sets them up for disappointment if the other person is tardy. Sitting alone and waiting is experienced as a painful rejection. To prevent this humiliation it is necessary to be late. Lateness is a preemptive rejection of the other person before the latecomer has the chance to feel any pain or even any anticipation of pain. But what if both people have this complex?

Other people are late because they are indecisive. They are not sure what to do before their appointment, which way to do it, or when they should leave to be on time. They experience committing to a course of action as a destruction of the wonderful life possibilities that lie before them. Commitment is for them a sadness and a denial of plenitude. Commitment obliterates the pleasure of anticipation and augurs only disappointment. The result is that yet another person is left waiting in a Starbucks.

One good friend of mine is notorious for how he makes plans. He will wait until the last possible moment, and this involves redefining the word *possible*. If he is flying somewhere he might go to the airport with multiple flight reservations. He will make multiple dinner reservations for when he arrives, both within each city and across cities. Only as airline check-in is closing does he decide where to visit. The restaurant commitment will come later. Needless to say, he is almost always late.

One economically minded solution would charge people—how about $1 a minute?—who arrive late for meetings or events. But this is unlikely to work.

To cite just one problem, the latecomer is often the boss. According to one study, American CEOs are late for meetings 60 percent of the time. The Ecuadorian rate of CEO lateness might be higher. Who is to mete out and enforce the fine?

Furthermore latecomers will start treating the fees as a price for being late. They will assume it is okay to be late, provided they pay. Important people might agree to fewer meetings in the first place, to the detriment of corporate communications. Systematic latecomers will demand a higher bonus to cover their costs, thus weakening the force of the penalties. And should we want a departmental manager to leave an important phone call simply to be on time for a meeting and avoid the fine? We probably need to go back to the drawing board.

One study of a day-care center found that penalties for latecomers were usually counterproductive. Under the prior rules, parents were expected to pick up their children by a specified hour. After all, the day-care center has to close. It is not worth paying a nanny to sit around and watch a single child. And what if the parent is very late and the kid starts screaming for food or comes down with a fever? Sometimes parents were late, but for the most part they understood it was simply their duty to be on time. The day-care center then instituted charges for late parents. The charges suggested that being late, while inconvenient for the day-care center, was okay. It was obvious that the day-care center had a plan for parental lateness, albeit a plan that required financing. By now, the result should not surprise us: the rate of parental lateness went up significantly.

In our culture certain social graces are being lost, often because we aren't so sure of what is expected of us, given the behavior of our peers. For instance it is getting harder to get an RSVP for an invitation.

Wedding and event planners report the problem is on the rise. The busy often don't know when they will have time to relax, while other people simply could not be bothered to respond. Other people have emotional problems with commitment, even a small commitment, as discussed above. Evite.com notes that invitation response rates have been running about 63 percent. Many people decide at the last minute whether to show.

Part of the problem is "invitation fatigue." Imagine receiving ten or fifteen invitations a week; often the quality of the offer is difficult to discern. Is my invitation from the Council on Globalization a career-changing event or a waste of time? When in doubt, wait. Of course in the meantime the Council does not know if this means "no" or if I am considering the invitation. Often I don't know, either.

The Evite.com service, combined with e-mail, makes the problem worse. We receive many more invitations than before. Evite also lets us see who else has been invited and who has already accepted. There is now a greater gain from "wait and see." I will go if the very cute Jo Anne goes, otherwise not. Jo Anne in turn is waiting for my response, or more realistically she is waiting to hear from Biff.

If organizers make follow-up calls, this can worsen the problem. Everyone waits to RSVP, figuring they will receive a call in any case. After all, who wants to be bugged repeatedly for a single event?

Nonrefundable deposits work when we are willing to confiscate the money and risk losing friendships. That is how concert tickets are sold, but it is harder when we are dealing with friends.

Bob McGrew of The Cardinal Collective (cardinalcollective
.blogspot.com) has suggested a system of raffles. Give out tickets to
people who RSVP "yes" early on and at the event choose a winner. Mc-
Grew also proposed allowing people to respond with a probability of
acceptance, rather than a simple yes or no. "I will go with a probability
equal to 0.4." (Will people undershoot or overshoot with their expressed probabilities? I expect undershooting, so the host feels good
when the guest actually comes.) Allowing the process to reflect more
information might seem like a no-brainer, but it runs risks. Potential
guests who would otherwise give a definite answer might defer and
submit $p = 0.84681$. What should hosts do with the numbers they get?
Estimate a probability density function? Will that really make it easier
to figure out how much wine and cheese to buy for the reception?

Motivating latecomers or no-shows is hard for two reasons. First, the
event in question might not be held regularly. That makes it hard to set
a commonly understood policy or to establish precedents. Second, it is
difficult to either reward or punish people who do not come at all.

• • •

SOME PROBLEMS ARE harder yet. How might we motivate someone who knows much more about performance quality than we do?
Jerry Seinfeld once asked, "What is the difference between a dentist
and a sadist?" His answer: "Newer magazines." We all know that going
to the dentist hurts. But can we make it hurt less? And how are we
supposed to know how much it should hurt?

The dentist worries about her long-run reputation as a caring prac-
titioner, but that only means that she targets an average quality of satisfaction from her patients. She still will inevitably treat different
patients with varying levels of care. My worry is that the dentist does
not try hard enough to alleviate *my* pain. I would like her very best
care, but I probably receive only the average.

Behavioral psychology suggests that the duration of a pain has little bearing on our memory of how bad that pain was. Instead, we tend to remember how bad the worst pain was, and we also remember how much pain we experienced at the beginning and at the end of the experience. Patient reports, as they are filtered into the marketplace, are an imperfect indicator of dentist talent or dentist benevolence.

I have considered paying my dentist a bonus at the end of the visit, at least if I think she has done an especially good job. But then the dentist might put me through too *little* pain. "Fragmented tooth? Don't worry, you can ignore it." The most satisfied patients are not necessarily the patients who are treated the best. The dentist may target short-term satisfaction rather than long-term dental health.

If we keep the same dentist over the years, a periodic Christmas gift is not a bad idea. A less trusting patient might pretend to be a dentist or perhaps a litigator. I have mentioned how many friends and relations I have, hinting that many of them require dental work and thereby positioning myself as a potentially important business contact.

With my current dentist, I pretend to have no fear. At the end of the visit I say what a great job she did. I expect better performance by supporting her self-image as a good dentist and, since she is new in my life, I find high-powered incentives difficult to apply. In any case I do not have access to penalties. But she might someday get a Christmas gift (even though she is Hindu).

So no, I don't think I can control my dentist or receive the very best care. By giving up this quest for control, however, I might get care that is just a little better than average.

I encountered another difficult problem when I visited Marrakesh, Morocco. I had read about the "guides" and the touts, but until I arrived I had not fully understood the traps awaiting me. On every corner is a local offering himself as a guide.

Marrakesh is a beautiful and indeed awe-inspiring medieval Arabic city. The town's walls date from the thirteenth century. Inside the walls are jaw-dropping wonders at virtually every step. A wanderer will come across an ancient Koran for sale, a snake charmer, a jeweler, or a spice merchant. And no, the old parts of town are not primarily for the tourists. It is easy to find medieval Arabic dentistry practiced in Marrakesh, of course without anesthetic. This is not a popular service among foreign tourists.

But those same parts of the city, however lovely and intriguing, are a maze. The small alleyways and winding major pathways—all without signs—are virtually impossible to navigate without assistance. At least if you want to get back to your hotel by 6 P.M.

The fundamental problem was this: for most of the day I didn't want a local guide at all. But I needed a guide to get in and out of the maze. And a guide would have been useful to bring me to the two or three stores I wanted to visit, as opposed to the twenty stores the guide wanted to bring me to, to maximize his income from commissions.

Perhaps more importantly, having a guide keeps away trouble. When I walked around without a guide, I was pestered incessantly by all the *other* would-be guides. It was like choosing which giant leech should be attached to your head, knowing that the space will not remain empty. In Marrakesh the main purpose of the guide is, quite simply, to keep away other guides.

The guides don't cost much up front ("I am your friend. I love United States. I show you for free. Very good friend. No charge nothing"), but at the end of the day they ask for money. And I don't just mean ask—I mean beg, plead, cajole, and finally, if need be, demand with anger. Avoiding this spectacle—humiliating to both parties—is itself worth at least twenty dollars. In the meantime the guides bring their victims around to shop and generate kickbacks on their purchases. So we cannot expect the guide to do our bidding or bring us where we want to go.

The guide thinks we will just love seeing the carpet factory with its price markups, its unctuous tea-pushing proprietor, and lots of child labor.

So how should a visitor structure an "optimal compensation contract" for the guide? How can we avoid being ferried to stores we do not wish to visit? Can the end-of-day performance art be dampened if not avoided? Surely we cannot rely on the guide's "intrinsic motivation" to do a good job.

Sadly the problem is not easy to solve. We can pay the guide something up front, but at the end of the day more money will nonetheless be demanded. We can use the guide one day and promise repeat business if the guide does a good job, but the guide knows he is unlikely to see us again. Furthermore the guide still expects to earn more by bringing us to the carpet shop than what he will earn from our continued small payments. We might promise a large payment at the *end* of the day, provided the guide does not bring us anywhere we do not want to go. But will the guide believe our promise? Furthermore he might think we really do want to visit the carpet shop, and indeed some tourists do.

The problem with the guide is a bit like the problem with the dentist. In both cases we are poorly informed about how to achieve our ends. The guide knows more about Marrakesh than we do. Once we are out there in the alleys, we are at the mercy of the guide. It is not so easy to turn down the visit to the carpet shop, given that "it lies right on the way home."

The best bet? Some hotels offer "official guides," who are disciplined by the hotel to stay on their best behavior. But of course they are relatively expensive, since they are preferred by tourists who cannot cope with the difficulties of Marrakesh. And they require that you stay in a relatively expensive hotel.

The bottom line is this: that Moroccan carpet costs so much because the merchants know that the tourists have little idea what carpets are really worth. And few locals are intent on helping us rather than farming us for cash. The result is that the carpet merchant, directly or indirectly, is bidding for more of the guide's loyalty than we are. In this situation it is foolish to think we can exert much control.

. . .

IMPROVING THE QUALITY of meetings is one of the most difficult tasks in this world or beyond. The problems with meetings are numerous and severe. One survey listed "Rambling, redundant, digressive talk" as the main plague. How about ill-defined objectives, lack of takeaway decisions or task assignments, excess length, tardiness, interruptions, and "general waste of time for all parties concerned" as further negatives?

Yet meetings continue and indeed they are a growing part of how managers spend their time. A survey suggested that an average manager spends one-fourth of his total week in meetings. Upper/middle managers spend an average of two days a week in meetings. Some senior executives spend up to four days a week in meetings.

Does this sound familiar? Given those numbers, a Martian visiting Earth might conclude that meetings are highly productive and delightfully entertaining. Um . . .

The literature on meetings is spectacularly bad, perhaps because it is written by people who have attended too many meetings. I went to Amazon.com, typed in "meetings," and purchased their number-one listed book, namely Barbara J. Streibel's *The Manager's Guide to Effective Meetings*. This book offers such gems of wisdom as:

Explain the purpose of the meeting.

Ask if there are any changes to suggest [in the agenda].

Keep the discussion focused and progressing.

If those are her best ideas, she is exactly the same sort of person I hate having meetings with. Surely the hardheaded, no-nonsense economist can do at least a little better. I have heard of—or in some cases experienced—the following more radical ideas for improving meetings:

1. Make everyone stand up until the meeting is over.
2. Hold the meeting over the phone, even when everyone inhabits the same corridor. This cuts down on the chatter and the side conversations.
3. Give participants a chess clock to limit the number of minutes they are allowed to speak.

   The rule is simple: make each person run his clock as he speaks. The clock records how much time has passed. When the flag falls, the allotted time is up and the player loses the chess game or in this case loses the right to speak any further. Quiet parties could donate their spare minutes—by passing their clocks—to articulate and helpful others.
4. Monitor emotions during the meeting. This idea is channeled through blogger and polymath Randall Parker:

> Aided by tiny sensors and transmitters called a PAL (Personal Assistance Link) your machine (with your permission) will become an anthroscope—an investigator of your up-to-the-moment vital signs, says Sandia project manager Peter Merkle. It will monitor your perspiration and heartbeat, read your facial expressions and head motions, analyze your voice tones, and correlate these to keep you informed with a running account of how you are feeling—something you may be ignoring—instead of waiting passively for your factual questions. It also will transmit this information to others in your group so that everyone can work together more effectively.

In other words, buzzers go off when everyone becomes totally bored. I fear that if this device were in widespread use, I would never be allowed to attend meetings.

Another option is to price everybody's time. As participants enter the meeting room, they privately enter their annual salary into a computer. The computer then continually computes the total cost of the meeting, in terms of the value of time foregone. The meeting chair can then announce, "Okay, we've spent $1,500 of the company's money—what have we learned?"

I'm all for voluntary experimentation, so do try these ideas. Being a former chess player, I feel special loyalty to the clock proposal. Yet there is a reason why it is so hard to improve meetings. It is not just that the rest of the world is stupid and unjust, though often it is. Meetings serve valuable but hidden functions.

Meetings are not always about the efficient exchange of information, or about discovering a new idea. Many meetings only pretend to be aimed at such ends. In fact most meetings are a kind of trick, serving some end other than their stated purpose. Sometimes meetings are displays of power, designed to show which coalition dominates. In this case time "wasted" can be necessary. If one side tries and tries but fails to dent the coalition, meeting participants observe that the coalition is robust. It can be necessary to wear down the opponents of an idea.

A meeting also might give attendees the feeling of being insiders and in charge of decisions, of having perhaps some illusory sense of control. I have noticed this motive with special frequency in bureaucracies. But that means these attendees must have the chance to speak and offer their input. What appears to be a waste of time is an exercise in building and maintaining a coalition. Once people buy into the idea that has been processed by the meeting, they will implement it with more enthusiasm.

As I discussed above, rewards and penalties can backfire if individuals do not feel a sense of control. Meetings counteract this tendency by—in essence—taking the people who frustrate us and making them feel influential. (Should that make us feel better?) After all, everyone else sat around and listened to them. These meetings are so painful precisely because the goal is to give a hearing to everybody, not just to the people who know best or who get to the point most quickly. It is especially important to listen to the blowhards and the obstructionists.

Here is the bitter truth: in the medium and long run, apparently inefficient meetings bring workplace rewards and penalties to life. Meetings help us invest in our self-images as cooperators rather than scofflaws. Meetings also give people the social context they need to behave in line with those incentives.

Along these lines, a meeting can send information about status. Who speaks? Who didn't show up? Who found it necessary to praise whom? We can learn the inside workings of a workplace—or confirm our suppositions—by observing its meetings. A workplace with no meetings will suffer from confusion and social ignorance. Productive people must first have enough knowledge to orient themselves in the social setting of the workplace.

In sum, if we wish to understand meetings, we return to the importance of intrinsic incentives. A good meeting transforms some workplace problems from the Car Salesman Parable into the Parking Tickets Parable, but with Swedish diplomats, not Kuwaiti ones.

To be sure, many meetings are beyond repair. Once people walk in the door they are hard to control. Do you really think they will tap their chess clock every time they toss in a stupid interjection? One simple way to improve meetings is to limit their number and duration. But if we go down that route, we need other means to produce social orientation and the appropriate feelings of individual control. We should hold more company picnics. And ask everyone for written comments on the new business plan. One way to control meetings is just to stop having them.

* * *

BEHIND OUR THREE parables, and the practical advice, is a broader social lesson. It is not easy to get incentives right. No single central planner or government bureaucracy has a good chance of doing so. No single company will, starting from scratch, have much of an idea how rewards and penalties in the workplace should operate.

To the extent that private commerce succeeds, it is because we rely on long-term, trial-and-error experimentation. We borrow from other peoples' experience of what works and what does not. Many of the best ideas enjoy success, and they are copied by others. Businesses with bad reward systems tend to lose market share. The competitive process thus contains implicit wisdom about which carrots and sticks work best. Often we do not even know what we are doing or why when we structure rewards or penalties in a particular way. We just feel "in our gut" that we should not give teachers bonuses if their students get As.

One of the least-heralded virtues of capitalism is how it blends and melds different kinds and mixes of rewards and penalties. Capitalism is not just dollars, dollars, and more dollars. It is also the best system for mobilizing intrinsic motivations toward the greater good of mankind. And that includes allowing people a sense of control.

Capitalism is about knowing when to change incentives and about knowing when to stop thinking about money. The problem with Soviet communism was not just that healthy incentives were too weak, but also that bad incentives were too strong. For most people in the Soviet Union, the only way to have a decent life was to court the Communist Party. This pressure was always present and always overbearing. The choice was to be a total rebel—which usually led to a very bad end— or to court or at least tolerate power. Virtually every social and economic decision was influenced by this calculus.

Of course this was an unhealthy incentive, but that was not the only problem. It is less commonly understood that the Soviet Union offered less scope for incentive-free behavior than does capitalism. A state-controlled economy led to less play, most of all in the realm of creating and implementing new business ideas. Play was pretty much restricted to close friendships and family relations. The result was less creativity and less personal human investment in making our world a better place.

And that is a big reason why communism failed.

4

Possess All the Great Art Ever Made

OTHER THAN CONTROL, what do we really want? Economics is supposedly obsessed with money, but when it comes to applying incentives, the more important idea is that of scarcity. Scarcity refers to the fact that most of what we want is not in free supply. Of course, some scarcities are more important than others.

A good intuitive economist approaches a practical problem by asking "What is the relevant scarcity hindering a better outcome?" If we haven't posed this query, and assembled at least the beginnings of an answer, we may founder. For instance, we might make the mistake of throwing more money at a problem, when money is not what is needed. By identifying the relevant scarcity, we learn where to direct the incentives.

The scarcity idea goes beyond the simple fact that we would all like to have more money. As society becomes wealthier, the most important scarcities are no longer of material goods. In our highly civilized society the scarcities I notice most often are those of *attention* and *time*.

In the realm of culture, learning how to overcome those scarcities is worth more than spending a billion dollars on oil paintings. Let's say what we really find hard to achieve is a feeling of relaxation about our schedules. That is, we would like to be people who find the time to give attention to movies, paintings, sculptures, music, novels, and the arts and cultures of the world.

But it is not just a question of clearing our calendar, we also need incentives to follow through on our intended program of cultural consumption. So if we wish to learn more about culture and enjoy culture more, we need to learn where to direct the penalties and rewards. The twist is this: incentives are not just about influencing other people; incentives can be about overcoming our own imperfections. We need incentives to get ourselves to pay better attention, to care more, and to be more open-minded about new genres of culture. We need to apply the incentives *to ourselves*.

Our own personal imperfections are often a more serious problem than a lack of money. Especially in culture, money alone doesn't always get us what we want. Yes we can buy a notable Picasso portrait if we have $100 million to spare. But simply owning the painting is no guarantee of enjoyment. I have visited art collectors who keep some of their most notable works in the attic, in storage. I've seen such works allowed to fall behind the toilet. Lack of curiosity about one's paintings is perhaps the worst sin of all; perhaps a brilliant landscape hangs over the fireplace but no one ever looks.

The potential gain is from enjoying paintings and using paintings to improve our lives. If a person can develop a knack for appreciating creativity, and cultivate the right kind of open and relaxed attitude, even at a wage of $50,000 per year she is better off, in cultural terms, than a clueless billionaire.

. . .

SCARCITY OF ATTENTION means that at some point we simply do not care anymore. I am a fervent bibliophile, but I find it hard to read for more than eight hours running. That shrinks to four or five hours if the print is small or if the books are difficult. After five hours of music, or fewer, my ear becomes dulled. My favorite song becomes a headache rather than a pick-me-up. I do fine with Wagner's *Das Rheingold*, a 2-CD or sometimes a 3-CD set, but my attention lapses during *Die Götterdämmerung*, usually a 4-CD set. I love (some of) the music, but to be honest I am happy, not sad, when the performance is over. Two to three hours is my limit at an art museum, no matter how good the pictures. I get "museum legs," my back hurts, and I can no longer digest the pictures on the wall. I start to whine.

Every marketer understands the scarcity of attention. Why, after all, are stupid and uninformative commercials repeated so many times, if only to stick in our minds? Why are hotels selling room items, from towels to reading lamps? They know that you're a captive audience and have little else to pay attention to during your stay in the room. Why do publishers invest so much time and money into giving their books attractive covers and snappy titles? They and I hope, at least in one case, that catching customers' attention will cause them to buy the book. Attention needs to be grabbed precisely because it is so scarce.

And once a book is sold, will anyone have time to read it? About forty desired but unread books live in my house, not to mention those I wish to reread. I have a pile of more than twenty CDs I have never listened to. In a good month the pile might shrink to ten. Fifty others I have heard only once. And enjoyed. I've figured out how to work iTunes but have yet to find the time to download many of my favorite songs. The ninety-nine cents is not the problem when it comes to Marvin Gaye's "I'll Be Doggone." I live near the Smithsonian, which offers nineteen museums for free and includes, of course, changing exhibits. Most of the galleries are excellent. In relative terms I am an avid museumgoer, yet I get to only two or three shows a month.

Every year more than 200 movies are put out by Hollywood. I see about forty movies per year, plus DVDs, but I still miss many gems, especially from other countries. I developed a taste for Bollywood, but India puts out more than 800 movies per year, not to mention decades of back inventory. The typical Bollywood movie is more than three hours long. I dropped out of Netflix. The service was affordable, but I felt the unwatched DVDs on top of my TV set as an oppressive burden and a marker of guilt.

And if you live in Manhattan, Paris, or London, well, I don't see how you get anything done at all. When we consider the scarcity of attention and the scarcity of time, and their impact on human behavior, it is a miracle that any kind of common culture remains possible.

Original paintings aside, most cultural experiences are remarkably cheap, especially if you live near a major city and have an Internet connection. *The Collected Works of William Shakespeare* sells for as little as $5 on eBay. A complete recording of Beethoven's thirty-two piano sonatas—highlights of his oeuvre—goes for as little as $40. Wonderful architecture usually can be seen for free. Public or educational libraries offer most of the world's literary treasures for nothing. We can have remarkably rich cultural lives without owning a Vermeer, and indeed no private individual currently owns a verified Vermeer.

So doing well with culture is not primarily a matter of money. Nor is it a matter of formal education. Educated people tend to "get more" out of culture, especially high culture, but education is not itself the key to their enjoyment and learning. In today's world, going to high school, college, and graduate school is correlated with intelligence, persistence, and other qualities that make culture easier to appreciate. But this was not always the case. No one in Beethoven's audience, or in sixteenth-century Florence, had a Ph.D. or, for that matter, a master's degree. Yet many of those people loved culture with a great intellect and a passion. Philosopher George Santayana remarked that the ancient Greeks were the uneducated people in European history; yet in cultural terms they did pretty well.

For the most part, getting a lot out of culture is an acquired skill, dependent on periodic immersion in a cultural environment, combined with a willingness to learn and adjust. We can do better with culture by focusing on two principles of self-management incentives:

1. Start by asking "What is scarce?" Is it time, attention, or, in the case of owning a Picasso, money?
2. Admit that we don't care as much about culture— at least any particular piece of culture—as we like to think we do. If we force ourselves to "enjoy everything in the proper way" we often end up avoiding culture altogether. Let's come to terms with our imperfections and turn them to our advantage.

But those principles sound so general and so abstract. How might we apply them in the busy, noisy world we live in?

• • •

LET'S SAY WE'D like to visit the Metropolitan Museum of Art, but don't fancy ourselves experts. The museum has seventeen separate curatorial departments (most would be worthy museums in their own right) and owns more than two million pieces of art. It stretches for four city blocks and has three levels. In the antiquities section, a single room might have more than fifty objects. We could spend weeks wandering from one gallery to the next. How can we get the calmest, richest, and most complete experience of what the museum has to offer?

Most people spend more time reading the placards than looking at the art. Even glancing at every description requires a separate eye movement, which breaks our attention. Just reading the dates and sources of each artwork could take up a whole visit. Many visitors look closely in the first few rooms they visit, then their eyes glaze over and they tune out. Furthermore, we soon realize that many of the men and women visiting the museum are, in their own ways, at least as beautiful and as interesting as the art. The art has a difficult time holding our attention. There is not enough incentive to look more closely.

An art historian, or perhaps a schoolteacher, would tell us to read a book on art history or perhaps search the Web for information before coming to the museum. These strategies can be useful, but they do not address the fundamental problem of aesthetic overload. In fact, reading more may *worsen* our overload. Our reading is likely to make us realize how many treasures lie before us, but we will be no better suited to cope with them. We don't have the time or energy to take in all the wonderful displays.

The art critic tries to make the viewer a better person. This sounds good—after all, who is opposed to "better people," or people who are better informed? But it is not necessarily the way to solve the problem, which is fundamentally one of attention and interest. In contrast to the art critic, our Inner Economist starts with the recognition that our attention is scarce and works with that constraint. I therefore recommend the following:

1. In every room ask yourself which picture you would take home—if you could take just one—and why.

   This forces us to keep thinking critically about the displays. If the alarm system was shut down and the guards went away, should I carry home the Cezanne, the Manet, or the Renoir? In a room of Egyptian antiquities, which one caught my eye? And why? We should discuss the question with our companion.

   To put it crudely, we must force ourselves to keep on paying attention. Ranking the pictures focuses our attention on our favorites. It also focuses our attention on ourselves, which is in fact our favorite topic. Me, me, me. It sounds crude, doesn't it? But if the "Me Factor," as I will call it, is operating against the art rather than working with it, our love affair with museums won't last very long.

Finally, it is fun to imagine ourselves as thieves. Theft is exciting, and we value objects more highly when we can think of ourselves as owning them. That is also part of the Me Factor.

Of course, we must ignore the carping of the sophisticates. Well-educated critics may claim that pictures cannot be ranked, value is multidimensional or subjective, or that such talk represents a totalizing, colonizing, possessive, postcapitalist, hegemonic Western imperialist approach. All of those missives are beside the point. When it comes to the arts, dealing with the scarcity of our attention is more important than anything, including respecting the artists.

2. Pretend we are shopping for pictures on a budget.

We are probably better trained at shopping than looking at pictures. So we might do some basic research on prices (e.g., surf the Internet or visit an auction house). How might $20 million be spent at the Met?

Or how about $500,000? The smaller budget forces us out of the market for major paintings and into niche areas. This exercise will again focus our attention, force us to clarify our intuitions, and improve the quality of our viewing. The shopping question puts the Me Factor, albeit unobtrusively, back at the center of the experience.

Viewing art at an auction house is useful for learning about prices. In New York City, November and May are usually the best times for advance viewings of auction material. But local auction houses hold viewings throughout the year. Typically the quality of the selection is worse than at a pre-culled art museum.

Nonetheless it often makes for a superior viewing experience, if only because of the prices and the shopping and browsing mentality that the setting induces.

3. When visiting a blockbuster exhibit, skip room number one altogether.

There is too much human traffic, because people have not yet admitted to themselves that they don't care about what is on the wall. Maybe you don't care much either, but you will care more by relaxing the pretense.

4. At the end of the visit, ask which paintings stuck with you.

Did you find yourself thinking back on the Munch, the Pollock, or the medieval tapestries? A week later ask the same question. *Then* go read about those artists or that period. That is a more useful procedure than reading about the art in advance.

These recommendations flow from the general principles from above. Our time and attention are scarce. Art is not that important to us, no matter what we might like to believe. So we should stop self-deceiving and admit to ourselves that we don't just love "art for art's sake." Our love of art is often quite temporary, dependent upon our moods, and our love of art is subservient to our demand for a positive self-image. How we look at art should account for those imperfections and work around them.

Art has a social role in addition to its aesthetic value. We like art for how it complements our self-images and our relationships with others. Being by nature a lover of theory, I enjoy identifying with the grid-based abstract art of Piet Mondrian more than with Victorian fairy painting. When I was single, I would have been suspicious if a date of mine loved Monet above all other artists. He is a wonderful painter, but I would fear that she would find my tastes—which include Bruce

Nauman and Jeff Koons—too strange and that I would find her too mainstream. And yes, I take special pleasure from seeing a Louvre exhibit that my friends have only read about. That is again the Me Factor.

Sometimes a museum will rehang its permanent collection but call it a special exhibit. Attendance usually rises even when the pictures have not materially changed. Visitors also pay closer attention. They feel they are getting something special and thus they care more about it. *They* feel special, and that motivates further interest.

Admitting the Me Factor is a big advantage. Keeping up a pretense to the contrary means that museum-going becomes a burden. In the longer run, this leads us to restrict our visits and ultimately to resent the art and find it boring.

Sometimes we go to a museum and find all or most of the art unattractive no matter what strategy we follow. Why might this be? First, not all museums are good. Second, not all pictures in good museums— even first-rate museums—are worth looking at. Most artists, even famous ones, painted a fair number of stinkers, or okay but mediocre pictures. Museums nonetheless hang the pictures because the name of the artist brings prestige and it attracts more visitors or perhaps donors. Even if we are sometimes wrong, we need to feel comfortable saying the painting stinks.

This is not a (-nother) diatribe against contemporary art. It is often the Greek and Roman statues that are the most boring displays. Many displays of antique ruins are, well . . . ruined. Most contemporary art will fail to pass the test of time, we just don't always yet know which pieces. Or a museum may need to spend donor money in an area in which it can never hope to excel or where other museums have already acquired the major pictures. The Getty Museum in Los Angeles tries to buy fine Rembrandts and Old Masters, but most of the best works in these areas are no longer for sale.

Most generally, keep in mind: museums are not put there to make you happy. Can I repeat that? *Museums are not put there to make you happy*. Perhaps that sounds strange. After all, we are used to institutions that try to make us happy. McDonald's tries to make (some of) us happy, at least the regular customers (I prefer Chipotle). If a majority of customers want a different kind of French fry or fish sandwich, McDonald's will try to figure that out and switch. As for the minority of people who wanted the old food, some other restaurant may step into that void. Restaurants, like most private businesses, depend upon customer satisfaction for their livelihood.

But museums do not depend on "customers" or ticket buyers to the same extent. For a typical art museum, ticket receipts do not cover one-tenth of the cost of their operations. For McDonald's, customers account for virtually all their revenue; I am not aware of anyone donating money to a fast-food chain, but perhaps it has happened.

Museums are far more dependent on their donors and sometimes on government subsidies. Direct subsidies are a more important source of museum income in Western Europe, not the United States, so let us focus on donors. For most American art museums, donors account for well over half of the yearly budget. The real influence of donors is much stronger, since donors are also the most important source of donated or lent paintings and sculptures. Donors may also volunteer, help museums organize exhibits, or use their contacts to borrow artworks from other museums. After all, most important museum donors are wealthy and influential people. A museum that does not make its donors happy will shrink in importance, relative to museums that are more donor-oriented. The incentive for a museum is to please donors.

Donors do not want exactly what visitors want. Visitors want that the museum be fun and easy to use. Donors are more concerned that the museum confers status upon them in the arenas of high culture, high society, and perhaps high finance. Donors like fancy receptions, which is why museums hold them.

In part, museums care about visitors for indirect reasons, so that their donors do not feel they are supporting an empty house. But the interests of viewers and donors do not in general coincide, and we should not expect the viewers to win out. (Note that zoos, which typically rely more on admissions and less on donations than do museums, tend to be designed for fun.) Consequently not every museum is easy to use. Don't expect it to be. Get used to that. Work around it. Use mental reframing to make the museum more like institutions that are geared to satisfy us.

A very different problem of attention arises when we look at the same image too many times. Overexposure can cause disappointment with paintings or museums, especially at the top tier. At some point we stop caring and we even lose the ability to care. We are all supposed to love the *Mona Lisa,* which is often described as the world's greatest painting. Is it? I tend to prefer late works by Titian, landscapes by Giorgione, or portraits by Velazquez. But honestly I don't know how good the *Mona Lisa* is, and I don't even know how I could know.

I am not invoking postmodern skepticism about the arbitrariness of objective value standards. *I don't even know how much I like the painting.* When it comes to the *Mona Lisa,* it is hard for any American or European today to look at the picture with fresh eyes. Cultural commentator James Twitchell has offered a list of just this kind of overexposed artwork:

1. The *Mona Lisa*
2. Grant Wood's *American Gothic* (you know, the "Cornflakes" picture)
3. *Washington Crossing the Delaware*
4. Michelangelo's *David*
5. *Whistler's Mother*
6. Munch's *The Scream* (we will see whether its recent theft, return, and damage will resurrect its aesthetic oomph)

I'll add Gilbert Stuart's portrait of George Washington—which adorns the $1 bill—to the list. Nor am I happy about the "Mondrian bag" and the "Mondrian shampoo." Twitchell goes further and suggests that: "Monet, Picasso, Degas, Cezanne, Gauguin, and van Gogh are just on the edge of becoming cliches." Economists call this phenomenon "the tragedy of the commons." A tragedy of the commons occurs when individual actions, taken together, destroy the value of an asset or resource.

In this case the lost value is the surprise and power of art. Many sources, such as authors, editors, and advertisers, display an image, but in the process the famous starts to look ordinary. The result: the surprise is used up too quickly and the images bore us rather than astonish or delight us. It is like having too many people tell us the same joke within a week's time. No matter how good the joke, at some point it ceases to be funny and perhaps even becomes annoying.

The exhaustion of surprise is less frequently a problem for music, which taps into our nervous systems more directly. But still I cannot hear John Philip Sousa's "Liberty Bell March" without seeing a giant foot come down from above, setting off the beginning of *Monty Python's Flying Circus*. Liszt's "Hungarian Rhapsody #2" reminds many people of *The Bugs Bunny Show*; fortunately I rarely watched that cartoon. But a few childhood viewings of the TV show *The Lone Ranger* have ruined Rossini's *William Tell Overture* for me.

The importance of context suggests that results of the test of time are difficult to predict in art. An image can appear powerful in 2006 but by 2030 may be trite. The colors of the French impressionists do not appear dissonant or shocking to the modern viewer; they come across as conservative and pretty. After Led Zeppelin, Gene Vincent no longer sounds like such a hard-rocker. The dinosaurs in Steven Spielberg's *Jurassic Park* were a special-effects revelation at the time and they delighted millions of moviegoers. Today they appear amateurish, as if they came out of an underfunded computer game from Eastern Europe.

Alternatively, other images and other cultural outputs gain in power. The fusion, funk, and general chaos of the late recordings of Miles Davis were a mystery to most jazz critics at the time. They could not understand why he would abandon bop or silky trumpet playing for what sounded like noise. Those recordings are now seen as seminal forerunners of jungle, trance, rap, and ambient music. Winslow Homer was often considered a lightweight in his time, but we moderns catch his sophisticated references to race issues and his obsession with human mortality.

These connections imply a concrete lesson for how we should view art museums. We should view paintings repeatedly, but especially after we have spent time with other artworks. The best way to better understand one art museum is to go see another art museum with a related but not identical collection.

These calculations will change once frequent repeat viewing becomes possible at home. Someday technology will make possible high-quality reproductions of first-rate paintings. Living with Picasso's *Mademoiselles d'Avignon* or van Gogh's *The Potato Eaters* would fundamentally change how we think about art, and of course we would find it easier to look at great and powerful images all the time.

Currently, copies of masterworks are unreliable, low in quality, and are produced one at a time. What if we could scan paintings by Rembrandt and create thousands of good copies just as we record compact discs full of music? Reproductions in books (at least so far) do not pick up textures or reproduce colors faithfully. They are no substitutes for an accurate, detailed, and life-size three-dimensional holograph, hanging on the wall and indistinguishable from the real thing.

At first museums would be reluctant to license copies of their masterworks, but public pressure would mount and sooner or later the images would be released. The original paintings might retain a sacred status in our hearts, but more practically we would not need museums to experience the highest artistic achievements of the human race. If we wanted, a perfect image of Raphael's *Madonna* could hang over the kitchen table.

Some masterpieces would become more overexposed. In the longer run our aesthetic standards might change. Probably the most valued paintings would be those that stand up to repeated exposure without losing their surprise value. Paintings based on the idea of "perpetual mystery"—like the *Mona Lisa*—might not win this competition. Pleasing shapes and colors, which are more basic in their appeal, might fare better. Just as mass reproduction (i.e., recording) moved music from "classical" styles to the more visceral rock and roll, painting might evolve to genres with more direct emotional impact and fewer intellectual fine points. Painters could earn more money and fame by appealing to the masses.

I believe that most people would find it oppressive to live with "great art," as that concept is traditionally understood. They *prefer* the inferior rendition. They like the tepid landscapes they put on their walls. Even if the prices are low, there is less of a mass market for perfect Caravaggio reproductions than meets the eye. For most people, the dark and brooding paintings of a seventeenth-century, possibly criminal, bohemian painter who favored the homoerotic don't do much for the Me Factor.

Just because people go to museums, don't think they want to own a copy of a Caravaggio or even a copy of a Leonardo. In this new world, owning perfect reproductions of those objects would probably not bring much status value.

How many of these people, right now, own a recording of Johann Sebastian Bach's complex *The Art of the Fugue*? As of May 2007, the bestselling version of that piece of music was #5,072 on the list of Amazon.com's sales rankings for music. Sales are slow, and it is not because everyone already owns a copy of this masterpiece.

For better or worse, most people prefer art that makes them happy, or that they think will make them more relaxed. Look at market prices.

Paintings with light colors sell better than paintings with dark colors. Happy portrait subjects sell better than widows. Horizontal pictures are easier to hang over fireplaces and sofas. Here are a few other market regularities:

1. Landscapes can as much as triple in value when there are horses or figures in the foreground. Evidence of industry usually lowers a picture's value.
2. A still life with flowers is worth more than one with fruit. Roses stand at the top of the flower hierarchy. Chrysanthemums and lupines (seen as working class) stand at the bottom.
3. There is a price hierarchy for animals. Purebred dogs help a picture more than mongrels do. Spaniels are worth more than collies. Racehorses are worth more than cart-horses. When it comes to game birds, the following rule of thumb holds: the more expensive it is to shoot the bird, the more it adds to the value of a painting. A grouse is worth more than a mallard, and the painter should show the animal from the front, not the back.
4. Water adds value to a picture, but only if it is calm. Shipwrecks are a no-no.
5. Round and oval works are extremely unpopular with buyers.
6. An eighteenth-century François Boucher nude sketch of a woman can be worth ten times more than a comparable sketch of a man.

In each case the Me Factor is at work.

. . .

ART MUSEUMS ARE just one part of our culture and just one medium for becoming a cultural billionaire. Reading is no less a source of depth and inspiration; indeed it seems that more modern lives have been transformed by novels than by paintings or sculptures.

But how should we "attack" classic novels that seem boring on first inspection? One Amazon.com reviewer noted that William Faulkner's *The Sound and the Fury* ". . . is like an ungrateful girlfriend. You do your best to understand her and get nothing back in return." Many other readers, perhaps less figuratively, feel the same way.

Keeping in mind our fundamental principles—the scarcity of time, attention, and giving a damn about art—here are a few tips for reading. The key is to keep ourselves involved, rather than to mimic the behavior of a literature professor at Yale. If people stay interested in a product—like their favorite computer game—they will put in the extra time to understand it better.

That said, try some combination of the following:

1. Read some middle or end chapters first. They may pique your interest. Don't obsess over sequence.

2. Read through the novel the first time, following each voice or character, skipping passages as you need to. Get interested in at least one character, even if the rest is a cipher. Then reread the book as a whole in order. This works especially well for multi-voice works such as Faulkner's *As I Lay Dying*.

3. Read the first fifty pages three times in a row before proceeding. Make sure you understand at least one part of the book.

4. Don't be afraid to skip over material and return to it later. This is necessary for the first fifty pages of Joseph Conrad's *Nostromo*. Material that destroys our interest in a book is negative, no matter how important its contribution to plot or character development. Since you're not going to remember all of a book anyway, don't feel so guilty about skipping over some key parts. Laugh and cackle while you skip, if you wish.

5. Read through the book the first time without stopping, but do

not try to understand what is going on. Treat it as investment in the book, akin to driving to the bookstore, rather than as a forum for judgment. Then try the book again, but with some idea of where matters are headed.

6. Start by reading some of the secondary literature on the tough book. Again the goal is to get ourselves interested. I don't like CliffsNotes, if only because they are boring and they deaden the works they summarize. But don't be afraid to "go low" when looking for help. Do not start with exalted literary critics unless you are persuaded they will be either involving or entertaining.

7. Take notes on the names and most important features of the major characters. Write these notes on the front leaf of the book or somewhere else accessible.

8. Give up. Recall the words of Samuel Johnson: "A man ought to read just as inclination leads him; for what he reads as a task will do him little good."

Some combination of these tricks almost always works. Most generally, we enjoy reading most when we feel we are in control (there's that word again). Harold Bloom tells us, correctly, that we should read: "to strengthen the self, and to learn its authentic interests." It is hard to meet those ends if we go through the book feeling like hopeless idiots.

One common recommendation, found in Mortimer Adler's *How to Read a Book*, is to read the book out loud to oneself or to others. This approach can be wonderful, but I am suspicious of it as a general recommendation. It usually brings a bimodal result, meaning we either love it or we give up on the book altogether. When we are speaking aloud, it is harder to slough off a poorly understood phrase or sentence. Both the ear and the eye are regulating our reading. Some people will respond by trying harder and delving into the book more deeply; others will simply give up. Unless we are superb readers to start with, we end up feeling like fools virtually every stanza. Reading aloud is a risky strategy, best used by the truly committed.

Keep in mind that books, like art museums, are not always geared to the desires of the reader. Maybe we think we are supposed to like tough books, but are we? Who says? Many writers produce for quite a small subsample of the eligible reading public. In earlier times many writers wrote to please or attract patrons, including government nobles. Today many writers work in universities and seek tenure. Or they are wealthy enough (if only because of a helpful spouse) that they write to please themselves or to please a small and specialized literary clique.

Sometimes we will just want to say "forget them." But other times we have our own reasons for wanting to understand these literary classics. The worst thing we can do is to assume that we are supposed to like the book and then feel guilty when we don't. That will push us away from reading. *Very often we are not supposed to like the book* so far as the author is concerned. When James Joyce wrote *Ulysses* he was not pandering to reader tastes.

Think of learning to like the book as a kind of trick we play on the author. If you wish, take delight in playing the trick and subverting the author's purpose and desired audience. Get back at the author and make the book part of your plan and your life understanding, not the author's.

• • •

OFTEN THE BOOK market is not really about books at all. According to one survey, more than a third of London book customers admit that they sometimes buy books "solely to look intelligent." Of course the percentage of true fakers is higher, and those fakers are not limited to London. One out of every eight young people surveyed admitted that they sometimes buy books "simply to be seen with the latest short-listed title." Short-listed for the Booker Prize, that is. (Given the visibility of the Booker Prize in the U.K., I suspect that this is more of a British than an

American phenomenon, but we have our trendy books too, including Oprah's picks.) For those over fifty, only one in twenty will admit to similar motives of showing off; after all, the young are more peer-conscious.

It is difficult to find systematic evidence on how many Americans actually read the books they buy. I have heard editors suggest that the percentage is no more than half. Jerrold Jenkins, also from the publishing trade, claimed that 57 percent of purchased new books are not read to completion, but the method behind this number is unclear. No study subjects book buyers to actual surveillance, so any numbers rely ultimately on self-reporting. Of course to the extent people favor image over substance, self-reports are precisely the source we cannot trust.

"Reading a book" is also a matter of degree rather than kind. How many chapters were finished, and did the reader pay attention the entire way through? Here is an Amazon.com review of Henry Miller's *Tropic of Cancer*: "This book is one of the worst books I have ever read. I got to about page 3–4."

The percentage of true readers depends on the nature of the book. Self-help books are usually bought to be read; there is otherwise little status attached to owning the title or showing it around. Few people read coffee-table photo books, and indeed they are not intended to be read. I find the text in these books is often surprisingly good, perhaps because the author—or more importantly the editor—feels no need to pander.

My candidate list of largely unread bestsellers includes Camille Paglia's *Sexual Personae* (how many finished that chapter on Edmund Spenser's *The Faerie Queene*?), Thomas Pynchon's 784-page *Mason & Dixon*, and Stephen Hawking's *A Brief History of Time*. Note that Hawking in 2005 followed up with an easier to digest "sequel" called *A Briefer History of Time*. The first book had only 208 pages; the sequel is pared down to 176 pages. As one nerdy T-shirt reads: SO WHAT PART OF QUANTUM MECHANICS DON'T YOU UNDERSTAND?

Sometimes it would be better if some people did not read classic books. When the book doesn't fit into their vision of the Me Factor, the results can make us wince. Here is an Amazon.com review of William Golding's *Lord of the Flies*:

> I am obsessed with *Survivor*, so I thought it would be fun. WRONG!!! It is incredibly boring and disgusting. I was very much disturbed when I found young children killing each other. I think that anyone with a conscience would agree with me.

Or try this take, again from Amazon.com, on one of my wife's favorites, Thornton Wilder's *The Bridge of San Luis Rey*:

> Basically all that happens is five people die on a small bridge and then the author goes on to discuss these people's lives. What a BORE. Unless you're some philosophical nerd, you will not enjoy this book at ALL. If I was the author of this book I'd tell myself to get a grip on the real world.

• • •

WHEN IT COMES to improving our purchases of music, we must grapple with The Love of the New.

Most people buy only very recent music, rather than mining history for the very best music of the entire past. Niche fans—such as in classical music—tend to focus on recently released or rereleased recordings, even when the composition is old. Like everyone else, they are excited by the new arrivals in the marketplace. Some people really do just want Verdi and Mozart, but this is part of the reason why classical music is well under 5 percent of the market in recorded music releases.

Every now and then rereleases make a big splash. The Beatles' catalog was rereleased circa 1976, and many of the songs were hit singles again. But such successes are the exception and not the rule. Buddy Holly's "Every Day" was one of the most charming songs of the

early 1960s. James Brown's "Bewildered" was some of the most powerful two minutes of music of the twentieth century. Both are accessible
and easy to appreciate. Yet there is no push to rerelease either song on
a widespread basis to compete for hit status. There are plenty of rereleases, including recordings by these artists, but they are targeted for
sale to a relatively small number of aging baby boomers or collectors.
No one tries to make these songs major hits again.

Presumably music company executives do not think that either
song would bring in much additional money. The profits would not be
worth the marketing expenditure.

Most of the music in the United States is bought by people under
thirty years of age. I can assure you that most of these people do not already own these songs. Most older music is simply not on their radar
screens.

But why not? Buddy Holly and James Brown are *great*. Okay, some
of you may be thinking that Tyler is an old fogey. Maybe Buddy Holly
and James Brown are, on reflection, totally "lame." That is a matter
of taste. But there isn't much music being rereleased—with an aim
toward hit status—from 1969 either. Nor from 1970. Nor from 1980.
Nor 1990. Get the picture? The phenomenon goes well beyond the
possible defects of my favorite older songs. It can't all stink. Buyers
want the new. Why? I look to the Me Factor. Music is about identity.
It is also about a *differential* identity.

The problem with old music is simple. *Somebody else already liked
it.* Even worse, that somebody else might have been one's parents. Or
grandparents. I believe that Grandpa's fanship is less offensive than
that of the parents, but it is hardly cause for youthful cheer.

The moment that Elvis became popular with older people—when
he returned from the armed services—he lost his cachet with the
young. He was no longer a rebel. The young people of 1975 (I know, I
was one of them) considered Elvis to be a crooning fatso, comparable
to Wayne Newton and suitable for old ladies who visit Las Vegas. He

was one step above Lawrence Welk or Liberace. It was much later that I heard the Sun Sessions, and I started seeing Elvis as a salacious carrier of African-American ribald blues culture and an important musical revolutionary.

In many cultural markets—most of all in music—many of the buyers seek artistic secession. That means liking something new, or at least liking something that will appear new to one's peers. This secession does not occur every year. If Nirvana reaches peak popularity in 1994, people who start listening to "cool music" in 1995 need not reject Nirvana. Nirvana is associated with the school class one year ahead and of course with slightly older siblings. While youthful feelings toward the slightly older are decidedly mixed, there is a strong element of emulation and some degree of toleration. The two groups simply are not that different. Nirvana can remain cool one year (or more) past their peak popularity.

But as the years accumulate, Nirvana loses acceptable status. For the class of 2004, Nirvana was loved by the twenty-seven-year-old guy just finishing his MBA. Or perhaps they are loved by "the loser pumping gas," or by "the guy who runs the produce department." How cool is that? Suspicions set in. At some point Nirvana is no longer a good means of establishing one's identity. Many current fans of indie rock like Nirvana as an ancillary interest (after all, they did inspire later indie acts, such as The White Stripes), but few stake their identity on the group.

A few hipsters will invest their entire identities in the idea of "retro," such as wearing 1970s bell bottoms or listening to ABBA. But this is best thought of as rebellion against all other time periods, and a new and more radical form of difference, rather than wishing to take on the true vibes of the chosen retro attachment. Few of these people enjoy the TV shows or the cars from that same period, except as an occasional source of amusement.

For those who don't believe that music markets are largely about identity, how is it that musical tastes are so predictable? Take a girl who is twenty years old, grew up in suburban Connecticut, is Jewish, and majors in English at an Ivy League school. What is the chance that she is an avid partisan of heavy metal? Very small. Most likely her tastes run in the direction of "indie rock." She might also like classical music, especially if she grew up playing an instrument. She will cringe at the thought of country and western. Regaling her with the glories of Hank Williams, Sr., and early Johnny Cash will hardly make a dent in this armor.

Studies have shown that as individuals acquire more education, they increase their dislike of "low status" musical genres more than they identify with "high status" genres. One study of musical taste found that, of all genres, heavy metal is the most intensely disliked by the largest number of people. Rap came in second. Heavy metal and rap are the only two genres where more polled people "Dislike it very much" than merely "Dislike it."

Of course the more that some people reject a genre, the more that other people identify with it. Take a twenty-three-year-old beer-drinking gas station attendant in Oklahoma who did not attend college. The best bet for his taste is country and western music. Make him seventeen and put him in central Michigan and the chance of intense heavy metal fandom and guitar worship goes way up. Smoking pot also has predictive power. Neither male is especially likely to enjoy REM, Beck, Coldplay, or the other icons of soft independent rock, or for that matter Mozart or Louis Armstrong.

It is not that white Michigan teenagers are genetically predisposed to like heavy metal. Their musical tastes serve to reaffirm who they are, who they are not, and where they belong in the world. If the Michigan teenager is black rather than white, rap probably will replace heavy metal in his loyalties.

And who are the people who like just about everything, from Chinese pipa music to Bach to Algerian Rai to Stockhausen to bebop to

1920s blues? They are either musical professionals or nerdy upper-middle-class professionals, usually with some experience living abroad. That's me. Sadly I am no less predictable than the Grand Rapids stoner.

Even most musical cosmopolitans could reach further in their quest for the new. Country and gospel are generally popular in the United States (they are two out of the three most favored categories), but they are not beloved by those who claim to be musically tolerant and who like many genres. When asked, cosmopolitan listeners are far more likely to express loyalties to Latin music, jazz, blues, and rhythm and blues. In fact, cosmopolitan listeners—as measured by how many genres they claim to like—have an especially strong *dis*like of country and gospel, compared to the American public as a whole.

In other words, few of us escape the need to rebel against something. This is, as you might have guessed, a way of establishing a sense of being in control.

Music markets are obsessed with finding the next popular means of rebellion because young buyers dominate those markets. There was a time when the world was poorer, allowances were smaller, and parents had greater control. Before the second half of the twentieth century, teenagers did not buy most of the music in this country. For that reason, until the 1950s, music had less to do with rebellion.

For some perspective, here is some of the top-selling music circa 1951, 1961, and 1971.

1951: The soundtrack for *Guys and Dolls*. Mario Lanza. Yma Sumac. The Weavers. Les Paul. Tony Bennett.

1961: Bert Kaempfert. The soundtrack for *Exodus*. Lawrence Welk. Judy Garland. But also: Elvis, Connie Francis, Brenda Lee, and Paul Anka. Teen tastes are on the rise, as were teen allowances. Connie Francis, of course, is a pretty tame signal of rebellion, but Elvis shook his hips on TV.

By the late 1960s—Herb Alpert & the Tijuana Brass aside—the music market is driven by youth.

1971: George Harrison. *Jesus Christ Superstar*. Janis Joplin. Sly and the Family Stone. Michael Jackson. Carole King.

It is an open question how Nirvana sounds to the class of 2004, or how REM sounds to the Midwestern stoner. Does the guy deep down like REM, but he can't bring himself to admit it? Or do his cultural predispositions make him simply unable to appreciate the music? He doesn't get the literary references and his hormones are screaming "thrash guitar" rather than "gentle, soaring harmonies." Maybe he never gives REM a fair listen in the first place, so he doesn't have a real opinion.

Given these points, we can return to the question of how to become a cultural billionaire. Just as Goth Boy has his reasons for rejecting Haydn, so do most of us have our reasons for rejecting other musical genres. As the case may be, we neglect bluegrass, Indian classical music, Top 40 pop, rap music, Renaissance music, Afro-pop, big-band jazz, or Mahler, depending on our backgrounds and our sensibilities.

To be sure, some of these obstacles cannot be overcome. I have found that most Americans simply will not and cannot develop a taste for the microtonal wailing of Egyptian pop. Prejudice is not the main obstacle; rather, the music sounds like noise to their ears.

But many of our reasons for rejecting different musics are purely identity-driven. They can be changed by a shift in our personal orientations. We need only to take on a broader and more cosmopolitan set of concerns. These musical rejections are—in aesthetic terms—unjustified and silly. Most of the reasons for those rejections boil down to the Me Factor.

Some readers might protest. Many of us have tried heavy metal and hated it. I don't like much of it myself. But the very best of just about any genre, including heavy metal, usually is quite good. And we don't have to start by moving into the genre we like least. If heavy metal nauseates us, we can try the Louvin Brothers (bluegrass), Art Blakey (bebop), gamelan music from Bali, or Josquin (sixteenth-century Renaissance music).

If we can transcend the Me Factor, if only a bit, a remarkable quantity of first-rate music will stand before us. Simply slipping the disc into the stereo and listening once may not produce a new love. Listening ten times may not suffice. The key is to believe—sincerely—that this new music *means something to me and to my life*.

That can be hard, but it is in fact the cheapest alternative before us for generating wonderful new music. The Beatles are not getting back together again. Brahms is dead. Composers will not return to Baroque style in large numbers. It is we who hold the power of "the cheapest possible artistic revolution" in our hands. We need only will it. Imagine that if in one year the world produced 200 brilliant symphonies, 5,000 amazing pop songs, 300 first-rate CDs of jazz, and 5,000 mind-blowing ragas. And that is just a start.

That is nothing compared to what is already out there—unbeknownst to most of us—and what can be discovered on relatively short notice. We need only be determined to make ourselves cultural billionaires. When it came to strolling through an art museum, the key was to mobilize the Me Factor to make ourselves interested. For music, which is more readily at our fingertips, it is more likely we need to tone the Me Factor down a bit, so we become more open to new styles and genres.

. . .

BUT WHEN TO let go? When should we release the hold that a particular piece of culture, or a past style or genre, has upon our lives? After all, if we grew up listening to Count Basie, isn't it a kind of treason to jump to Merle Haggard and Brian Eno? Aren't we denying the very core of our being and perhaps our loyalties to region, race, religion, and family?

We can ask similar questions about our attachments to individual cultural experiences. When should we finish a book we have started? In this regard I am extreme. If I start ten books maybe I will finish one of them. I feel no compunction to keep reading. Why not be brutal about this? Is this book the best possible book I can be reading right now, of all the books in the world? For me at least, the answer is usually (but not always) no. Whatever is that best possible book to be reading, I am willing to buy it or otherwise track it down. Most other books don't make the cut.

I walk out of many movies, especially if I go alone. I go to many movies expecting to walk out, indeed *wanting* to walk out. I would like some idea of what the movie is about. Some of this curiosity is for my research, as I have written on the economics of film. Certain movies are so popular or so famous that none of us want them to remain a mysterious black box in our cultural experience. I'd like to get a feel for this movie and I don't always want to wait for the DVD or suffer the small screen. Knowing about the movie from what others tell you only goes so far. But do I really need to see the *end*? I can either guess how it turns out or read a review. For me the first half of Clint Eastwood's *Letters from Iwo Jima*—not a bad movie—was enough.

If I can manage to walk out of one movie, I can see parts of other movies that same day. One day I saw parts of four movies. I was happy, not frustrated by the experience. Three of them were better than I had expected, although apparently they were not good enough.

Sometimes I will see a movie that ends at 4:00 but schedule an appointment or a phone call for 3:00. I expect to meet my commitment. If the movie is really good—better than I expect—then I am in trouble. But it is a nice kind of trouble to be in. It means that *seeing the rest of the movie is better than anything else I could be doing in the world at that moment*. That's impressive. If that is the scenario to be worried about, I feel I am sitting pretty.

Economist Robert Hall once said something like: "If you haven't ever missed a plane, you spend too much time waiting around in airports."

This way to cultural riches requires more of the Me Factor—you don't have to pay attention for as long as the producer of the art form wants you to. But we cannot behave this way in all matters and at all times. In many cases we wish to honor our previous commitments, even if it isn't out of respect for the author or filmmaker.

We have bought expensive tickets for the theater. A sudden headache means we no longer feel like going. The economist might urge us to stay home, scolding that "sunk costs are sunk." Sunk costs has become economist jargon for *treat bygones as bygones*. We won't get our money back by going, and if the show had cost nothing, we'd probably have skipped it anyway.

Yet in that setting many of us feel guilty about having spent the money. We go to the show, determined to make good on our financial commitment and our self-image as a devoted lover of the arts.

This tendency is quite general. We eat more when we have paid for an all-you-can-eat buffet, compared to when somebody is treating us. Yet the food is free in either case and what we spent in the past should not matter. Nonetheless we feel we have to "get our money's worth." In another context, many couples have more mutual commitment when they make sacrifices for each other, compared to when everything comes easy. We value what we have to fight for, which is one reason why a woman might play hard to get.

We all encounter such issues of commitment, but how to resolve them? When should we treat the past as irrelevant and when should we stick by previous plans? When should we stay true to a cultural investment? The answer, again, lies in better understanding the Me Factor.

We use our cultural decisions to support or help create stories about what kind of person we are, what kind of marriage we want, or what kind of job we aspire to have. The most important of these narratives concern—can you guess?—ourselves. My personal story is that of a curious intellectual nerd polymath, loving husband and stepdad, and music lover and collector of Mexican Outsider Art, among other qualities. For better or worse, I've never much bothered with "pillar of the local community," "ardent political activist," or "suicide helpline operator." Sometimes I change or bend my narrative, but for the most part I invest in the stories I already have and extend them. Even when I pick up a new cause, I look for continuity with previous interests and commitments.

So if our stories matter, the past matters too. No good narrative jumps around every moment or moves onto a completely new course with every twist in the action. A story achieves force by linking past, present, and future events. Valuing our stories means giving credence to our past decisions and narratives; this means we will often honor sunk costs. Bygones are never truly bygones. By honoring past investments, and our past cultural attachments, we are building up a narrative and a self-image.

Sometimes our current actions confer redemptive value on past actions and prove that our previous sacrifices were not in vain. We go so far as to invent new ends, so we can see our earlier investments as part of a coherent pattern. We invent new justifications for our causes, especially when previous commitments otherwise stand to look foolish. Rightly or wrongly, many pro-war commentators redefined the case for attacking Iraq once weapons of mass destruction were not found.

So we now have a means of deciding when to go to the theater with a headache. We should go, and respect our previous investment in sunk costs, when we have a chance to strengthen beneficial narratives. We should not go—thereby cutting loose from our past just a bit—when the visit would support harmful or wasteful personal narratives.

A beneficial narrative is one that supports our happiness and the well-being of our community; a harmful narrative does the opposite.

So if the theater-ticket holder needs greater follow-through in life—he is forty and cannot commit to a long-term relationship—he should get out of bed and visit the theater. Headache be damned. If the ticket holder is an art snob, perhaps he should relax and break out of that narrative. He should nurse his headache and stay home to watch *Lost* or *Veronica Mars*.

Some economists will tell us that if we must honor sunk costs, we should do so when the cost of this behavior is relatively low. Stay home from the theater with a splitting headache but not with a hangnail. But this advice fails to appreciate what commitment really means and how we demonstrate it. It is our willingness to make significant sacrifices—to venture out with a bit of discomfort or pain—that gives our stories meaning. The narrative benefits of going to the theater are often highest when we are making the greatest sacrifices.

With this point in mind, let us circle back to whether we can become a cultural billionaire by being more of a musical omnivore. The broadening of our personal identities through this path will involve some very real costs. Listening more to a new musical genre might mean listening less to the music of our childhood or listening less to the music we share with our best friends. But those costs also signal our commitment and give meaning to our new and more cosmopolitan cultural self-images.

Is the new and broader cultural identity worth it?

We might look to the psychological research on "status quo bias," which shows that people tend to overvalue goods, services, and identities simply because they already own or possess them. If we give people drinking mugs in laboratory experiments, they will value the mug twice as much, or more, immediately upon receiving the mug. Just because the mug is "theirs." Similar loyalty effects have been replicated under a variety of conditions and for a variety of different goods or attachments. We are to some extent captured by our possessions.

Human beings have probably evolved this protective tendency to cement love for their families and close friends. Of course love and attachment are admirable qualities, but we need not and should not value the status quo so much in every sphere of life.

The general presence of a status quo bias means that most of us are probably just a bit overinvested in our previous cultural attachments. So to return to whether it is worth it, cultural broadening—and a dalliance with some new musical ideas—would do most of us some good.

Another answer is simply to punt on whether a shift in cultural or musical identity is worth it. This is a chapter on how to become a cultural billionaire, but hey, it's a free country. If you don't want to become a cultural billionaire, well, perhaps you are busy becoming a billionaire of some other sort. The other chapters may come in handy for those endeavors.

5

Look Good at Home, on a Date, or While Being Tortured

I FOUND THIS dialogue striking:

"You treat me like property."

So said a woman to her man. His reply?

"If I treated her as if she were my property, after all, it means that I would take care of her, protect her, and treat her well above all things not in my possession."

Suddenly, I realized the look on her face did not reflect the combusting happiness within me. Then I realized my error. We are all self owners, she as much as I. But let's say I were treating her like property. That raises the extremely important issue:

"Do you mean public or private property?"

I recommend that my readers do not raise this question to their partners. It is not the best means to a happy romance.

There is an important issue here, and it is the subject of this chapter. We would all like to look good, and in a wide variety of settings, including on the job and in our friendships and romances. Your Inner

Economist knows that how you appear is not just your clothes or your health or even just what you say. It is the total of all the signals you send and how well you tailor those signals to your audiences.

A signal, as economists use that term, is a simple concept. We signal every time we incur a cost to send a message about ourselves to the outside world. Signaling is a kind of personal advertising. We signal when we wear fashionable clothes, when we go to the right postgraduate school, and when we send the right color of flowers. The cost or difficulty is the whole point of signaling, and it is the reason why signaling sends an effective message. If flowers were free, or everyone knew the right kind to send, most women would not be very thrilled to get them. If everyone could work his or her way through Harvard Business School with ease, and choose the right advisor, the degree wouldn't mean so much.

Keep in mind that many signals are to some extent hidden messages. They are not completely explicit, or at least they should not be, if they are to be effective. They are signs of something that only the more interested or the more aware will read. They are usually partly covert or indirect. And that makes signaling difficult to execute. We wish to get a point across with signals without, well, appearing that we are trying to get a point across with signals. We don't want to look like we are boasting, or trying too hard, or needing to climb the ladder of success. We want to look like the kind of person who is so successful that he or she doesn't obsess over signaling.

A Dr. Rangel, a well-known blogger and M.D., offered this recipe for impressing a woman:

> Wine her, Dine her, Call her, Hug her, Support her, Hold her, Surprise her, Compliment her, Smile at her, Listen to her, Laugh with her, Cry with her, Romance her, Encourage her, Believe in her, Pray with her, Pray for her, Cuddle with her, Shop with her, Give her jewelry, Buy her flowers, Hold her hand, Write love letters to her, Go to the end of the Earth and back again for her.

This, perhaps surprisingly, does not always work. Often the best way to impress a woman is to do something that impresses other men. Famous politicians—who generally do not have time to practice all of the above—face no shortage of romantic offers. They don't even have to be wealthy.

Some people—call them villains—are trying to look bad rather than good with their signaling. The bad guy in Bruce Lee's *Enter the Dragon* is a muscled fiend named Bolo, played by martial arts superstar Bolo Yeung. Before confronting his enemies in martial arts contests, Bolo smashes boards and cement blocks with his hands or with his head. His opponents flinch before the match starts. He breaks their necks while ignoring their blows. The point is that a weaker fighter such as myself couldn't even break a board with a hammer, much less my head.

Do you see any professional wrestlers named Smythe-Thomson?

These examples might seem to suggest looking good is superficial or trivial, not a matter of good long-term behavior. Let's get to more weighty matters.

One individual wrote an economic or "game-theoretic" analysis of whether to leave the toilet seat open or closed. He used complicated mathematical formulas to conclude that economizing hand motions is the key variable. In his account, we should leave the toilet seat "as is" when done. Why bother switching when the seat might be needed in that same position again, and you'll just have to switch back?

A more sophisticated approach, based on a longer chat with one's Inner Economist, would recognize that such matters should be arranged to please one's wife, and that usually means putting the seat down after use. It is a symbolic recognition of her value.

The economic idea of "signaling" refers to sending a message by choosing a costly action. I signal when I buy my wife flowers on Valentine's Day; I am not convinced she needs the blossoms in mid-February. I am sorry to say this to all you cheapskates out there, but the *cost* of signaling is the entire point. A fancy diamond ring goes further than flowers. A free piece of advice, no matter how valuable, does not have the same cachet.

Women have long valued certain objects—such as flowers and diamonds—that men tend not to care about. Resale or gifting value aside, I would not pay $200 for the world's finest diamond. Women value the objects as gifts, in part, *because* men do not care about them. If I bought my wife the complete DVD set of *Battlestar Galactica*, she would suspect me of selfish behavior rather than dedication to her, even if she grew to love the show. So, the best gifts are often those that we, as gift-givers, do not ourselves value very much. Such gifts show we value *the gift receiver*, even if diamonds really are a waste of money.

Love cannot be measured scientifically or directly, at least not until neuroscience dramatically advances. We must instead show other people all the time that we love them, and that means we look to send the right signals.

The signaling concept was discovered formally in 1973, when economist A. Michael Spence, later a Nobel Laureate, published his Harvard dissertation on the idea. Spence drew on his experience with education. It seems that many degrees, such as M.B.A.s and J.D.s, are valuable out of proportion to what people learn in school. Isn't most of business school just a useless grind? Spence put forward a hypothesis: getting accepted to Harvard Business School and surviving the toil identified talented and dedicated workers for the future. Employers seek to hire the successful students, even if those students learned nothing from those case studies of Hellmann's Mayonnaise. (Spence later became dean of the Graduate School of Business at Stanford).

The three-year M.B.A. is a valuable means of identifying talent. It does not suffice to give everyone a test and hire the people with the highest scores. Many general-aptitude tests are illegal in the United States because of antidiscrimination laws, but that is not the point. Doing well on a test is no guarantee of perseverance. The signal must be costly and grueling, otherwise it fails to sort out the best job candidates. Conquering the world of business involves much more than test-taking skills. Of all personal qualities, self-discipline is arguably the most important in predicting future business and academic success.

Sometimes signaling shows cleverness rather than self-discipline, such as when men try out pickup lines. So what are good pickup lines, or, as the Brits would say, "chat-up" lines? Or if that notion is too risqué, what are good, wholesome introductions at church dances? Pickup lines represent the ultimate in signaling; in fact they are nothing but a pure signal, unencumbered by any other possible motivation. A man on the prowl has an incentive to look charming, reliable, and somehow special, compared to his numerous competitors.

In short, the man should demonstrate his uniqueness, yet without appearing that he is trying too hard. This is tough.

Neil Strauss wrote a book called *The Game: Penetrating the Secret Society of Pickup Artists*. This 464-page tome is supposed to reveal valuable secrets about seduction, but instead it is an object lesson in the importance of natural talent. Strauss claims:

> I learned that the more unavailable you make yourself, the more people would want you. The more you say "stop touching me" or "I'm taken" or "you're just not my type," the more people would actually chase you. . . . A small example would be—this sounds awful to say, but it's true—if, say I tried to kiss someone and got rejected. I found that if I just turned my head away and ignored them for about five seconds, then turned back and said the same thing, most of the time they'd then go ahead and kiss me. It could be a punishment-reward thing, or it could be that people's first reaction is no, but once they've had a moment to think about it, they think, "Well maybe this guy's alright."

I am no master of the craft, but in most cases this is the worst romantic advice I have ever heard.

A pure "hard to get" strategy fails to satisfy what signaling theorists call—forgive the nerdspeak—"a separating equilibrium." In other words, it does not sort (or "separate") the winners from the losers. "Hard to get" is too easy for the losers to mimic. If success with women (or, for that matter, men) required only "hard to get," hermits would be in fantastic romantic demand. They are not. Nor is everyone trying to be a hermit.

You have to get noticed in the first place. I've played "hard to get" with Salma Hayek for years, yet this reticence has paid few dividends, not even a courtesy e-mail or party invitation. If she responds, I am ready to "back off," but with her I am going nowhere fast. Instead, the courting partner must know how to induce or court initial interest and then—possibly—when to back off, if indeed backing off is called for.

Investing in real estate offers an analogy. We all know that prices are going up and down, and then probably up and down again. The brilliant investors are those who know *when* to buy and sell. That is much tougher to figure out.

A proper application of "hard to get" is, well . . . hard to get right. That is precisely what makes "hard to get" effective, when deployed by a master of the craft. If a man tries a hard to get strategy and fails to finesse the nuances with the proper skill, most women will think he is stupid or a jerk.

Effort alone is not enough to succeed in finding the right partner. Women are remarkably astute at assessing a man's true capabilities, and vice versa, if only because we have evolved this way in our searches for quality partners.

One study suggests different results from the snake oil peddled by Neil Strauss and his ilk. Forty different pickup lines were presented to an audience of 205 undergraduates, 142 women and 63 men. In each "story" a man approaches a woman with a line; the readers rate the lines for their potential effectiveness. This is hardly high scientific method, but it does go further than Strauss's stories. The results confirm common-sense intuitions. Pickup lines involving jokes, empty compliments, and sexual references did not impress the raters. Pickup lines revealing helpfulness, generosity, athleticism, "culture," and wealth received reasonable ratings. In other words, the man does (relatively) well if he displays some valuable quality, or at least if he can show some chance that he has that quality.

Of course evaluating pickup lines in the abstract misses a big part of the skill. The real trick is not just what you say ("Hey baby, come visit my Steinway"—or should that be Bösendorfer?), but rather in having the appropriate dress and demeanor, plus showing an understanding of social context. If a man is pursuing a woman, endorsements from the woman's friends are a big help. So are private planes, Mark Rothko abstracts, and a string of gold records. All of a sudden the woman has an incentive to be interested. In other words, women usually respond to traits that are hard for "loser men" to replicate. Men, when looking for women, respond to accurate signals of looks, intelligence, education, social class, and interest in children. Men and women often seek different qualities in their partners, but the same logic of signaling applies.

• • •

IF SIGNALING IS the way to look good, and so get more of what we want, why don't we do it all the time? The problem is that signaling wastes resources.

"I want to show that Malaysians are capable of world-class efforts."

Those were the words of Nur Malena Hassan. This young Malaysian woman lived thirty-two consecutive days in 2004 with more than 6,000 poisonous scorpions. To prove her feat, the exercise took place in a shopping mall, in the city of Kuantan, about 160 miles east of Kuala Lumpur. Dozens of shoppers paused on their routes to view scorpions crawling over the woman's body. She slept, ate, and prayed toward Mecca in a glass room. (She was allowed to leave the room once a day for fifteen minutes.) She also watched DVDs during the trial; her favorite was *Spider-Man*.

The same woman, in 2001, had set a world record by spending thirty days with 2,700 scorpions. Nur Malena was stung numerous times, which caused her to lapse into unconsciousness. Yet she persevered. To her chagrin, one year later Kanchana Ketkeaw of Thailand spent thirty-one days in a glass room with 3,400 scorpions. It was necessary to revisit the task in tougher form. She noted correctly: "Having 6,000 scorpions is different from 3,000. It's just worse [sic]."

Nur Malena notes that the scorpions are more active during nighttime. At least scorpions do not usually sting unless they are attacked or stepped on. The key is for the human to keep his or her cool, and this feat requires practice. Nur Malena allowed herself to be stung by scorpions for more than five years, so as to get used to the idea and also to build up immunity for the stunts. During her second world record–setting trial, she was again stung numerous times. For a while she could not walk, but she did not pass out.

When we see wasteful or otherwise puzzling behavior, our minds should turn to the possibility that we are witnessing signaling. We all care what the rest of the world—and especially our peers—thinks of us. For instance, many young black children are afraid to get good grades, for fear of being labeled "too white" by the other school kids. Failing at school is one way of signaling "in group" membership. Clearly the failing student is not trying to sell out.

If we feel frustrated by the world, the chances are good that signaling is the culprit. Consider a letter to "Dear Prudie," the advice columnist at Slate.com, which read in part:

> Dear Prudie: I recently attended a bridal shower for a young
> lady. . . . When we were all there, the hostess handed out
> envelopes to all of the guests and asked each person to address
> the envelope to herself, in order to receive her thank-you note.
> As I had received my invitation in the mail, I could only assume

that she already had my address. I was shocked at this rude gesture, which said to me that the bride couldn't be bothered to write a thank you note after I had found the time to attend her event and purchase a gift . . . or am I just being picky?

—Wondering

"Why didn't we do that?" was all this economist could think. But alas, it is often a mistake to pursue efficiency at the expense of image. Prudie's response was that such behavior was simply gauche: "She is missing manners, finesse, and a mother who bothered to teach her any social graces."

Again, the cost and inconvenience are the whole point of signaling and the source of its value. Signaling tells us who is who in the social order.

Sometimes signaling games lead to inefficient escalation. There is a Keeping Up with the Joneses effect. Do you know the old joke? A wealthy man is defined as one who earns more than the husband of his wife's sister. If the sister's husband receives a promotion, the previously wealthy man might now be expected to work harder.

The point is not to abolish signaling—which is impossible—but rather to use signaling to our advantage. More importantly, if we understand signaling we will have a new patience and the fortitude to accept those social facts that we cannot change. Signaling, by its very nature, is hard to circumvent, outdo, or avoid. Signaling will irritate most of us, or penalize us, at least once every day of our life.

Signaling helps explain why successful people feel overloaded. So often the source of our frustration is signaling with "face time." Here is a problem my Inner Economist does not know how to solve. Maybe yours can.

People—and not only at work—get insulted if they are dealt with in a brusque or peremptory fashion, even when the issue at hand can be resolved quickly. Imagine a visiting professor comes to give a seminar, but I can't (don't want to?) find time for lunch. Lunch would have been idle chitchat anyway, but now the professor feels I don't value his research—or *him*—very much. Can you imagine such vanity? If others perceive our time as important, they want it all the more.

Our children judge us, not by how efficiently we support their process of growth, but rather by how much effort we put into parenting. "I'm sorry, Johnny, I know your Little League game is tomorrow. I have an important conference call. Take a cab." Don't even go there. And if you do, it won't help to add: "Don't worry, in the meantime I'll earn more and put the extra money toward your college education. Not to mention the higher 'present expected value' of your future bequest."

Are there solutions to this problem? After all, a day has only twenty-four hours and our faces have (one hopes) only one side. Some strategies do come to mind:

1. Pretend that some other privilege (hand kisses? birthday cards?) is extremely costly and is granted rarely. Offer this other privilege in lieu of large amounts of time.
2. Pretend to be busier than is actually the case. Let people believe—perhaps truthfully—that everyone else receives even less time. One must cultivate the appearance of always rushing.
3. Pretend that your time is *unimportant*. (NB: This may involve dressing down.) The hope is that no one will feel slighted if they don't get much time. Who feels slighted not to be given free thumbtacks? But there exists another possible outcome, in which the neglected person feels all the more insulted. After all, we are not giving away even our crummy, low-value time. And dressing down will bring costs of its own.

None of these tricks is likely to make the problem go away. There is only so much time in the day. Your Inner Economist can't change the laws of physics.

. . .

NOWHERE IS SIGNALING more important than in the family. Whereas direct cash incentives work only so well in families, signals are crucial in building family trust and cooperation.

Many individuals—including my wife—like to feel protected against every possible danger. If I do not want to buy a warranty, my wife considers it irresponsible. I am not expressing maximum commitment to the idea of safety. Furthermore if I don't buy insurance when I could have, I will have the narrative of a man who did not care enough and let something go wrong. Often buying insurance is about investing in a story about who we are and what we care about; insurance salesmen have long recognized this fact and built their pitches around it.

My colleague, economist Robin Hanson, argues that many protective activities are really about "showing that you care." What would we think of the parent who did not do "everything possible" to protect his or her children? What kind of man would tell his wife that he weighed costs and benefits before spending on an additional biopsy for her cancer? In the aftermath of Katrina, we are trying to rebuild New Orleans, not because we have made a trustworthy calculation, but because we feel obliged. No one wants to seem like they don't care about New Orleans, especially politicians.

An economic approach suggests we should insure only against catastrophes that would wipe us out. Small accidents are not worth the insurance premiums, especially since that insurance is unfairly priced. The company offering the insurance must cover its payouts or repair costs plus the costs of selling the insurance. Since the costs of selling the insurance end up passed along to the buyers, in the long run the buyer fails to break even. Some buyers will get lucky and come out ahead, but buyers as a whole will lose money.

To cite one simple example, we should refuse to buy most product warranties. For most people the money saved on premiums will be greater than the value of the repairs and replacements received. Best Buy and Circuit City earn high margins on those policies, which is why they push them on unsuspecting customers.

Most of us view insurance as part of how we live. Often a person buys insurance to signal and to express loyalty to commitments. For instance, a person might buy life insurance to signal caring and reaffirm attachments, not because the heirs will need the money. We might buy a warranty on our new kitchen stove to express loyalty to the idea of a secure home, immune from tragedy or catastrophe.

Buying insurance is often about image. The data show that the worst drivers are the *least* likely to have insurance. These people are careless when it comes to driving and buying insurance because that is their self-image. This runs counter to the usual "adverse selection" hypothesis from economics, which predicts—incorrectly—that the best drivers are most likely to forgo insurance because they need it the least. My wife wants to make sure I am not one of these people with a careless or reckless self-image and therefore she expects me to buy lots of insurance. I would be happy with a general rider covering large liability suits, but in fact we end up with much more insurance than that.

Refusing insurance and warranties may appear risky, but it is often, in reality, the more cautious course of action. We can spend the money saved on a safer car. The benefits of greater calculation are often indirect or hard to measure. But if we truly care about protecting our family, sometimes we have to look a bit uncaring.

Yet it is hard for me to win family debates by citing economic logic. The benefits of insurance are more visible than many of the costs. My wife insisted that we buy a warranty on repairs to our air conditioner. I don't have to tell you my stance on the issue, but nevertheless we bought the warranty. Lo and behold, the air conditioner broke again and the warranty paid off. I have heard about this case since; it is a more memorable anecdote than all of the insured or warranty-covered gadgets that did not break.

So, should we buy that insurance policy? It is not easy to strike the right balance between caring and calculation. When "showing that you care" is done only to get ahead or impress others, people will notice and conclude that one does not care much at all. So we should not apply economic logic to every possible caring or signaling decision. Do not pull out the pocket calculator. Obsessive calculation breaks down trust and challenges the glue that holds families, cultures, and even states together when catastrophe strikes. Do not try to figure out if we should help a city struck by a hurricane. Do not estimate daily the costs and benefits of marital fidelity. These are decisions lying behind us.

The best outcome is for economics to steer many but not all family decisions. We should use financial economics to guide our real estate investments or our retirement savings. At the same time, economics and specifically signaling analysis should not be seen as ruling most interactions within the family. Most of the time—and certainly in the home—keep your Inner Economist hidden deep inside if you want to look good.

Many popularizations of economics hit the reader over the head with economic principles. Professor Steven Landsburg, at the University of Rochester, tells us in his book *Fair Play* that "marital property is abhorrent" (p. 218), because it involves too high a "tax" on productive activity; in his view, why should his wife get half of what he produces?

If economic reasoning were recognized as in control, familial trust would splinter. "Doing the right thing" would be seen as contingent upon calculation. We therefore should reject economic reasoning for small decisions, such as "Should the toilet seat be left up or not?" It is more important to affirm basic loyalties to making other family members happy.

Silence that economist. Zip his mouth. Send him away to write his blog. Do not let him subject family decisions to "the optimal theory of principal-agent renegotiation-proof coalitions." Saying things like "marital property is abhorrent" just doesn't work at home. And your Inner Economist knows that.

The trick is to limit the scope of economics in family life without disgracing economic reasoning altogether. Economics has much to offer family life. For instance, if we are thirty-five years old, we probably should put most of our savings into U.S. equities (risky, but the expected return is 7 percent), and not T-bills in a money-market fund (liquid and safe, but the expected return is about 1 percent). The economist should insist. If we are investing $1,000, and our stocks are a bit unlucky and yield only 5 percent, over fifty years the expected difference in returns will amount to about $1,600 versus $11,400, a difference of about eightfold. That's a lot of money to leave sitting on the table.

That same economist might even have a good idea for allocating the TV remote control device. Let the children trade for it. But now we are veering dangerously close to the edge of the acceptable . . .

The more our families feel we are violating our commitments to care, the harder the reception that economic advice will receive. Economics appears dangerous precisely when it is presented as universal—"Bidding for the TV remote? That can't be good; such a practice would imply we need to trade for how many times my mother can visit."

Think of "the economics of the family" as The Truth That Dare Not Speak Its Name. If you are the economically informed member of your family, or perhaps even an economist, don't flaunt it. Hide its universal nature or widespread applicability. Do not present economic wisdom as a matter of principle or as a general way of thinking about life. To look good at home, make all economic points in purely specific contexts. Don't prattle on about incentives or signaling as all-powerful means for understanding the entire world.

• • •

ONE OF THE fundamental questions in life is how much we should invest in showing that we care. My colleague Robin Hanson, mentioned above, has made this question a central feature of his work. It is also a central feature of his life. Robin is a forty-six-year-old former computer scientist turned economist. He is a wonderful father with two smart and lovely boys. Robin cares. Robin's boys know that he cares.

But Robin has studied signaling behavior for a long time. And anyone who studies signaling behavior for long enough will be repulsed by social hypocrisy and will be tempted to become some kind of intellectual radical, maybe a revolutionary, maybe a more peaceful eccentric, and this has happened to Robin. When it comes to showing that he cares, Robin wonders why it isn't enough that he cares. Robin wonders why he has to signal in all the traditional and indeed very costly ways. Robin is what I call a social revisionist.

Robin has strange ideas. He pays $200 a year for the privilege of having his head frozen when he dies, if indeed that turns out to be possible. He looks forward to life in the very distant future and believes that he will be thawed out just for the heck of it, or perhaps because a future rich man just wants to have an interesting conversation about mankind's past.

Robin believes that betting markets should be used to rule many human affairs, including government policy. We should bet on which policies will maximize national income, and governments should institute the policies that the betting markets show as most likely to succeed. Robin claims the money we spend on health care is a waste. Since doctors kill as many people as they save, we would live just as long without them. That sounds crazy, but the data show no correlation, either internationally or domestically, between health-care expenditures and life expectancy. Robin believes that we are headed toward a "robot economy" with rates of exponential growth exceeding 300 percent a year. Yet the wages of labor may fall below subsistence, leading to widespread poverty for those who do not own capital.

No, I am not ready to drink the "Robin Hanson Kool-Aid," but Robin's views are a challenge that any social thinker should face. Unless you agree with Robin, you need to explain how you can justify and live with all of the waste from your signaling.

My other friend and colleague Bryan Caplan put it best: "When the typical economist tells me about his latest research, my standard reaction is 'Eh, maybe.' Then I forget about it. When Robin Hanson tells me about his latest research, my standard reaction is 'No way! Impossible!' Then I think about it for years."

Robin believes that signaling is virtually everywhere. Indeed he comes close to a "single cause" theory of human behavior. In his reductionist view, the competition for survival is fierce. Species are honed by millions, indeed billions, of years of evolutionary competition. Why waste resources on anything not devoted to genetic fitness?

The crude prediction is for only two kinds of activities: reproducing and trying to reproduce. Of course humans spend only a few hours a month, on average, having sex. So, in Robin's view, the rest of our activities must be devoted to furthering our genetic fitness. This usually means signaling, or, in other words, taking costly actions to show that we are fit mates.

Robin does not hold the preposterous view that all activities are consciously directed at mating. If a ninety-year-old granny is sitting in her chair and knitting, she is not thinking about how this will attract a man. But the activity is, according to Robin, probably a byproduct of some other biological "program" that evolved to make us successful breeders. For instance, the woman may enjoy knitting because, in the past, nature rewarded women who practiced their dexterity with their fingers; perhaps it was a useful skill for caring for their families.

If we like the arts, this capability has evolved to signal that we are caring beings and that we understand, or can create, complex symbolic messages. It only feels like we love the arts for the arts' sake; in fact the charade is part of the point. If our love for the arts is to attract others—that is, to *fool* them—we have to feel our passions as sincere.

If we enjoy sports, perhaps we were programmed to show off our skill at hunting. If we discriminate against others, perhaps an "in group" orientation was functional in hunter-gatherer society. And if we seek sexual intercourse, well, we know why that is. A creature that didn't enjoy sex wouldn't get very far in the Darwinian struggle. We are even programmed to think that the highest forms of sex are spiritual or exalted in nature, if only to show just how seriously we take our relationships.

Robin is a modern-day Gnostic. He is convinced that the reality we observe is a mere shroud for some deeper set of truths. Hardly anything is as it first appears to be, and just about everything in the social world is guided fundamentally by instincts to propagate our genes. In Robin's view, our evolutionary programs are often ill-suited for modern society. Robin therefore sees the human race as facing a crisis of survival. Technology has changed society more rapidly than our biology and our instincts can adapt. For instance, we appear to be programmed to seek revenge against enemies. This may have been efficient (at least for the individual, if not for the world as a whole) when the major weapons were spears and stones. It is far more dangerous when the arsenal includes nuclear missiles and biological warfare.

Robin wants us all to be more aware, and that is why he is a social revisionist. He is himself a good-natured, slightly nervous, but always enthusiastic sort of guy. Behind his scientific exterior lies the heart of a preacher, who wishes to thunder against social hypocrisy and dishonesty. On a more practical level, Robin doesn't see why he ought to be signaling all the time. He even imagines a future world where we are all "computer uploads" and no one has to signal anymore. Just read the other person's program. Everything explicitly stated, nothing covert, seductive, or mysterious.

Doesn't sound like much fun to me, though some would say my view of signaling is more conservative, less idealistic, and even jaded. I do not think signaling can go away, or that railing against it will have much positive impact. People, and society, can change only so much. But having been infected with the Robin Hanson bug, I cannot help wondering *what is the preacher—Robin—trying to signal?* How does a tendency to rail against hypocrisy help propagate human genes?

• • •

ROBIN CARES FOR his family, but what about people who are trying to start families in the first place? Which signals should they send?

Enter Megan from California, one of my favorite blog writers; she posts at www.fromthearchives.blogspot.com. Megan, a beautiful woman in her mid-thirties (I once met her at a bloggers' party), placed a personal ad on Craigslist in 2006. The question: how should she describe herself? This is, of course, a problem of signaling, and it challenges the notion that signaling is necessarily indirect.

Here is her ad:

> You know who I really want to date? I want to date one of those twinkly-eyed grad students with a beard. Not necessarily one who is in grad school, or one with a beard, but one of those thoughtful, cheerful, feminist guys who amble through the halls of their department and who are so kind in office hours (sadly, not the type of office hours I could write letters to *Penthouse Forum* about). Those guys have dogs, and do projects, and are often Jewish, and play sports. The pretty ones are graceful and slightly bow-legged, but the key is the smiley eyes.
>
> Thing is, I don't meet guys like that here. Where are you, bearded grad-student guy? Don't tell me you are home with your wife and baby, 'cause that doesn't help. Are you out in the field, tracking Sudden Oak Death? 'Cause if you came home to me sweaty and hungry, I would have dinner waiting and join you in a cool shower. Have you just not had time to call, because you finally got scheduled for some time on the telescope? Well baby,

you can wake me when you call; I would never want to miss talking to you. Are you at some local café, working on a proof? I would meet you there, but bring a book so I won't interrupt you. Just smile at me when I get there, so I can watch the lines around your eyes crinkle.

(Fellas, if you are not a bearded grad-student guy, or you aren't sure if you are but you went to grad school, please do not write me just because I mentioned sex . . . Hope to hear from you, bearded grad-student guy!)

Should Megan ask for something so specific, or should the ad simply cite a few general features about Megan (attractive, smart, employed), to attract as many male respondents as possible?

Megan chose specificity. Most men are not the "bearded, graduate student guy," especially given Megan's age. I describe Megan's search method as "Make Him Fight Dragons." Under this approach, the advertising woman does not trust the process of subsequent back and forth—e-mails, meeting for coffee, etc.—to yield a good catch. So the woman becomes very specific in the ad about what she is like. The number of responders goes down and the woman hopes that the right man will see through her character and choose her. The woman places a great faith in the ability of her Mr. Right to spot the ad of The Matching Woman.

In other words, highly specific ads are, for better or worse, an attempt to limit one's subsequent choices. They also preempt rejection by scaring off many potential suitors in advance. "Don't get close unless you are sure you can tolerate a big dose of me" is the implied message.

A highly specific ad can also be a demand for the near impossible. The woman placing such an ad seeks the most romantic story imaginable. She is requesting a man who is infinitely perceptive and appreciative of her nature and who is full of love for her virtually from the get-go. This will attract some men, and put off others.

There is another method that Megan did not try, namely inducing as many high-quality men to respond as possible. I call this approach The Honey Trap. It sounds as straightforward and guileless as could be. The woman should find the relevant "bottleneck" for eligible men and use the ad to get them through it.

Consider one example of how this might work. Sometimes the bottleneck is that many men won't write in for fear the woman simply won't write back. If a woman doesn't mind lying (or writing a lot), she could promise to respond to all messages, one way or the other. More men will write in and be drawn through the "bottleneck."

What else? How about photos, or at least links to photos? How about a video link to oneself chatting? The man will judge the woman—as "wife material"—by the photo. But since the woman has to pass the "looks hurdle" anyway, this won't rule out many true eligible men. If a man doesn't see a photo, the odds are he thinks the woman doesn't pass his test. It is not just that the ugliest women might be the least willing to post a photo; for most men the default assumption is that any given woman doesn't pass the man's looks test.

Not every man is looking for a supermodel. But *every man in pursuit of a wife wants one who doesn't look a certain way or set of ways*. When I was single I didn't want women who wore Prada, for fear that those women would not be intellectual enough. Posting the photo is more likely to signal that "the woman looks okay."

After that, under this view, the rest of the ad should be accurate, signal high intelligence in fairly straightforward fashion, *but otherwise be bland*. The woman can say one or two idiosyncratic things, perhaps to attract a few ardent admirers, but the woman should not be too edgy or scare anyone off. In other words, don't let men rule themselves out because of fears that may or may not be valid. If a smart, searching man likes how a woman looks, sees she is smart, and expects a response, he will write to her.

Look at it this way. Neither the women nor the men know exactly what they want, even if (especially if?) they think they do. Both sexes are error-prone and self-deceiving. The key is simply to induce further contact, some e-mails, and perhaps a meeting. So the self-description in the ad should involve some ambiguity rather than a perfect description of the self. The ad placer cannot trust the ad readers to do the proper sorting and selecting just from how they interpret the ad. So the placer has to attract a lot of responses and then do the sorting through subsequent interactions, like meeting for coffee.

So what kind of personal ad should an individual place? It depends. If the woman (or man) is a sharp chooser and willing to bear the costs of rejection, and also the costs of processing, she should go with a bland ad. If the woman hates being rejected, she thinks the men are the better judge of a good match, and she demands the highest levels of perception, a highly specific ad would be better.

• • •

IT IS TOUGH to look good while you are dating. With all the attendant fears and anxiety of competition, it is a wonder we ever manage to persuade someone that we are presenting "the real me." Indeed it is always very hard to convince people when we are telling the truth once there is doubt in the air.

Let us say that an innocent person has been captured and threatened with torture. He is, for whatever reason, entirely willing to betray the information he holds. His primary goal is to avoid pain. Imagine, for instance, that he was vacationing in Lebanon and was mistaken for a CIA agent. He is now sitting in an empty room, tied to a chair, surrounded by bald men with moustaches, half-shaven beards, and bulging muscles.

How should he present himself? He would probably want to signal that he is an unknowing innocent, in the hopes of earning a speedy release. After all, terrorist groups of this kind do not kill everyone they capture. But of course the bald men do not believe him. After all, wouldn't a hardened CIA operative pretend to be an American tourist interested in beaches, Arabic music, and Middle Eastern cuisine?

This shows why any truth-telling strategy is hard to pull off. The liars will seek to copy that very same approach. After the captors mutter to each other in Arabic, they start to torture him. They commence with punching and slapping. In the distant corner he sees drills, pliers, and garden shears, all neatly arranged on a table. Now there is some powerful signaling.

To be sure, there is a small literature on how resist torture. It tells people to adhere to a rigid ideology or religion, think of their comrades in peril, be polite to one's captors, and play mental games to keep some notion of being in control, if only concerning the smallest matters. If the victim can keep control over which shirt to put on, or which portion to eat for breakfast, he is more likely to withstand the torture. American POWs in Vietnam found that they could resist with some success by volunteering personal rather than classified information, and by falling back upon deceit and distortion if the interrogator got too close to a military truth.

I am not sure these claims have been empirically verified in a scientific manner. But the evidence shows that many people do withstand torture. For instance, French court records from 1510 to 1750 showed that of 625 tortured people—faced with drowning, drawing, and crushed joints—more than 90 percent refused to confess. Many U.S. prisoners in North Vietnam signed written confessions and condemnations of American military policy, but few of them offered up useful information, despite years of torture and mind games.

Nonetheless, that advice is not very useful for the innocent captive in Lebanon. He is not trying to withhold information. In fact he would be very happy to break. He simply wishes to be set free.

The key is to find some behavior pattern that differs from that of a trained operative. His torturers look experienced, so presumably they have some idea of how the real CIA or Mossad agents behave under pressure. Ideally he wants to do the opposite, and thus signal that he is not in fact a trained agent.

But it is not easy to appear innocent and unknowing. Most agents go to training school and take classes on how to avoid or withstand torture. Some presumably have received professional schooling on how to maintain a disguise. They would try to do exactly what our captive is trying to do. The question is which behavior the torturers would interpret as an unlikely tactic from a truly determined CIA trickster.

So what are his options?

1. Break down immediately, beg for mercy, humiliate himself, and say whatever he can about what they want to know, even if he must make something up.

   This is not a bad try, and it is what many of us are inclined to do anyway, if only through nervous collapse. But it will not be very convincing. After all, if this does correspond to what torturers would expect from an innocent, a trained operative would be instructed to do the same. Our innocent captive would look just like a tricky trained operative.

   Besides, if he talks right away, they might torture him anyway, just to see if his story changes. And since he doesn't really have any more to tell them, why should they stop? At some point he'll start changing the story simply in the hope that it will satisfy them. But once the story starts to change, they will continue to torture him to see which further permutations might spill out. For that reason, I have to vote against this otherwise tempting option.

2. Our innocent captive could go in acting tough, really tough. At the first sign of serious pain, he would start crying and switch to strategy #1.

   The thought here is that a real CIA operative would not start by acting tough. Most people are bad actors. If the terrorists can see the captive is a bad actor, they may let him off the hook. Of course the CIA operative really *is* tough. So the operative's attempt to appear tough, if indeed that was his strategy, will succeed easily, perhaps too easily. He won't look like he is engaging in bad acting. For him to mimic an amateur, the CIA guy would have to "act at being a bad actor," namely mimic Joe Smith appearing to be tough. That might be hard for him to do.

It is hard to be sanguine in the basic situation, but I consider #2 to be one of the better options.

3. Wait until they apply their "best shot" torture, and then talk. They will feel they have done their job and stop.

I cannot recommend this policy. First, I doubt if most of us can hold out so long. Second, it involves virtually no chance that they will stop early. The best shot is if this strategy collapses, however inadvertently, into #2.

4. First offer (or make up) compromising information to show disloyalty to the cause the torturers are fighting. The captive's profession of innocence will then be more credible.

Note that the terrorists do not have to believe the "concession" for this ploy to work. The pronouncements only need embarrass a real CIA agent with real CIA operatives. The captive could repeat "The Americans are imperialist pansies" and offer to tape this pronouncement for radio or Web broadcast.

The captive also might try: "I never met a CIA spy and never want to. Everyone says they all stink." Or "Let's cut the CIA budget." The torturers might think that a real operative would be reluctant to disgrace himself in this fashion. That might set the captive apart and help establish his innocence.

None of my friends would think ill of me for making such an admission under stress. But some of the friends and colleagues of the CIA operative might think the guy is soft, just as American POWs in Vietnam developed their own codes of how far they would go when they broke. Even if such admissions are the release-maximizing strategy for the real spy, some real spies might be reluctant to try it.

5. The captive could say he doesn't know anything, try to fight the torture, but break down when he can't stand it anymore. He can't fool them, so the best he can do is to actually "go through the wringer."

In economic language, the captive is stuck in "the pooling equilibrium," which means he cannot distinguish himself from a real CIA agent. Trying to deny his lot only makes him worse off. It confuses the torturers. To get over their confusion, they are induced to torture him more. (What else can they do? They are unlikely to be masters of inductive reasoning and Bayesian inference.) The best the innocent captive can do is to receive the treatment that would be meted out to a real agent. This is scary.

It is unclear that an innocent victim can do any better than #5. In related fashion, is there anything a captive could say to the United States authorities to avoid rendition to Pakistan?

Your unrelenting Inner Economist will extend the analysis further. How does the best answer depend upon the hypothesized motives of the torturers? If the torturers find torture fun for its own sake, this militates against #4. They don't so much care if the captive is a real spy or not. In that case the captive is probably stuck in scenario #5, so why should he humiliate himself?

Alternatively, the torturers might find their chosen occupation a laborious burden. They are torturing the captive only because they have been promised a bonus for making him talk. Numbers 2 and 4 are then more likely to succeed. So when they come at the captive with the pliers, he should look for either smiles or frowns before proceeding.

By the way, the difficulty of this problem has implications for the policies of the United States toward captured suspects. Some percentage of these suspects will be innocent or perhaps guilty of only minor infractions and not committed terrorists. But if we try to torture them, how can we tell the guilty from the innocent? It is not easy. That is one reason why torture should be used only as a very last resort, such as when a nuclear time bomb is ticking somewhere in midtown Manhattan.

Quite simply, it is hard to show other people, in a convincing manner, that we are telling the truth. In the meantime, file this problem under "Difficult to Solve" and stay out of the wrong cities.

Of course torturers are not the only ones who have a hard time getting at the truth. Studies suggest that the typical person lies at least one or two times in the course of a day. One set of self-reports measured an average of 1.5 lies a day, and of course since these people are regular liars their answers may underestimate the true rate of lying. So with all the duplicitous possibilites in signaling, do we have any way to get at the truth? Or does the fact that everyone wants to look good or has some ulterior motive hopelessly obfuscate things?

The standard stereotypes about liars are not generally true. Liars do not, on average, gaze away when they speak or fail to make eye contact. In fact some liars make excessive eye contact, if only to counteract the common expectation of how liars behave. Nor do liars seem to touch their noses or clear their throats at abnormally high rates, again contrary to the popular wisdom.

If liars have any detectable physical traits, they tend to move their arms, hands, and fingers less when they talk. Liars also blink less. When it comes to their speech, liars make fewer stumbles or grammatical errors than do truth-tellers. They are less likely to backtrack and go back and fill in parts of the story "they forgot," or "they got wrong," as would normal storytellers. Liars are devoting a greater percentage of their brain to the fib, and thus they shut down other functions, often subconsciously, to keep their concentration.

Liars also try not to make mistakes, for fear of looking like liars, or out of fear of seeming confused and thus drawing greater scrutiny. A normal storyteller is less likely to feel this inhibition and is thus more likely to stumble and bumble through the narration. In short, the liar is overly scripted. Bella DePaulo, who works on deception research at the University of California, Santa Barbara, noted of liars: "Their stories are too good to be true."

Some researchers believe that liars show telltale facial expressions, or "micro-expressions," as they are known. Paul Ekman, a retired psychologist from the University of California, San Francisco, has spent much of his career studying these cues. He claims that liars have telltale twitches, eye movements, pauses, and physical hesitations. But these motions are not usually easy to spot, even if we are paying attention and looking for them. For instance, social psychologist Mark Frank, a professor of communication at the University of Buffalo, has spent hundreds of hours watching slow-motion videotapes of crooks, killers, and liars proclaim their innocence.

Most people are bad at detecting well-crafted lies with any consistency. On average it appears that participants in experiments distinguish truth from falsehood only 55 percent of the time, just slightly better than a random result.

It often doesn't help us much to understand the body language of liars. Even if liars don't wave their hands much, it doesn't mean that people who don't wave their hands much are liars. They might be calm and collected by nature. Nor should we assume that Italian-Americans—who tend to talk with their hands—lie at lower rates than average. These features of liars may be statistically accurate, but they are broad, aggregate characteristics. They are not a guide to definitive judgment or anything close. In other words, just as in the torture problem, honest people find it hard to send off signals that show they are truly and definitely honest.

Lie detector tests are far from foolproof. The test itself stresses the innocent, and can induce lying-like stressed reactions. Guilty parties can learn how to fool the tester. More advanced technologies include scanning the brain with a high-density electroencephalograph machine, with 128 sensors attached to the face and scalp. After all, telling a lie can take 40 to 60 milliseconds longer than telling the truth and it may require new data-assembly strategies from the brain. Or we could measure blood flow in the capillaries around the eyes, using periorbital thermography. Researchers claim success rates of 70 to 80 percent.

Inventor James Larsson has attached electrodes to eating utensils, so that a host can ascertain whether a guest feels either very happy or stressed. Larsson intends his invention to help geeks—who cannot read body language very well—to date more successfully. It is more likely that such a technique, or related ideas, will be used in business negotiations. And hey, guys, let's play poker over at *my house* tonight . . . Whatever the virtues of these methods, we don't really have access to them in everyday life.

Some people—not usually professionals—can act as super lie-detectors and identify liars with an accuracy of eighty percent or more. One researcher, Maureen O'Sullivan, notes: "All of them [super lie detectors] pay attention to nonverbal cues and the nuances of word usages and apply them differently to different people. They could tell you eight things about someone after watching a two-second tape. It's scary, the things these people notice." These super lie detectors beat even the trained professionals, but only about one in one thousand of the studied subjects gave signs of such unusual abilities.

Most of us must look to simpler tricks to catch liars. The recipe is simple: to get at a person's real opinion, ask what she thinks everyone else believes. Drazen Prelec, who teaches psychology and cognitive science at MIT, refers to this method as "Bayesian truth serum."

The premise behind this approach is the following. If people truly hold a particular belief, they are more likely to think that others agree or have had similar experiences. For instance, if a man has had more than thirty sexual partners, he will more likely think that such behavior is common. After all, his life is one "data point," and that data point presumably weighs heavily in his mind. Most other people do not have access to that same experience. Furthermore the man with more than thirty partners probably knows a higher percentage of other people with thirty partners or more. This will further encourage him to make a high estimate of how many partners other people have had.

If we ask this man about his sexual history, he might be expected to lie and downplay his bed-hopping, especially if he is talking to a prospective date or to his wife.

But we can catch these liars off guard. They still tend to assume that other people have had life histories at least somewhat similar to their own. When we talk about other people, we are often talking about ourselves, whether we know it or not. Remember the Me Factor? It holds for gossip, or for answering questionnaires, as well. So we might ask our Lothario what he thinks other men are up to. If a man says he has had seven partners but he thinks the typical man out there has had thirty, watch out.

Another trick for eliciting honest answers is simply to ask for advice. When people tell us what *we* should do, their true selves, true desires, and true worldviews come to light. We love being the boss so much that few people can resist unveiling their true selves in this role.

• • •

THERE ARE WAYS of getting at the truth, and sometimes they involve a rejection of very obvious forms of style. Let us conclude the chapter with observations about what works not so much in interrogation rooms, but at the office or workplace.

Consider that the most impressive Japanese business cards are those that list only the person's name, and no title or affiliation.

If I were a spammer I might try the subject heading "NOT SURE WHETHER THIS IS WORTH YOUR TIME." Some people would be interested enough to read the message.

These are examples of counter-signaling. The Japanese business card doesn't suggest the person does no business; on the contrary, he is so successful and important at his work that no introduction is needed. Counter-signaling is when the very rich dress like bums. A metrosexual is so sure of his sexual prowess that he can act, dress, and walk like a so-called girlie man.

I received an e-mail message one morning with the not very promising heading, "Not a scam." Ha! I would have deleted it without looking, but instead I sought the anecdote for my blog. The contents?

> Face it, you're not getting paid enough for what you do
>
> http://www.silverstate.co.sy@click.net-
> click.net.ph/click.php?id=sicosyl
>
> to get off our database follow this link:
>
> jdefdmu s vgkitbaqizknh bdqdwxpoav w brfpu gotwzykprljsywaonqk

I hate spam but I couldn't help but admire the craftiness.

If a book lists "Ph.D." after the author's name, be wary. The author needs those letters to signal his importance. It usually means the author is not used to interacting with peers, is appealing to the gullible, or is making questionable claims. Stephen Hawking does not use those three little letters.

If your Ph.D. is from Harvard, try saying you went to school "Up near Boston." In elite British boarding schools it is considered desirable to receive either top marks or very bad marks. The stupid people are thought to be clustered in the middle. They tried to do well and failed. They couldn't figure out that it would have looked better not to try in the first place.

At most administrative meetings I refuse to wear a tie. In part I find the article of clothing physically oppressive. But in part I am showing that I am a tenured academic, and that my salary does not depend very much on the approval of any person in the meeting. I once heard my (former) dean say that a faculty member was not trusted "because he dressed too well." Everyone wondered just who that professor was trying to impress, or what other realm of achievement he was trying to enter. I wonder whether good academic dressers are more interested in political appointments or consulting gigs than in scholarship.

But counter-signaling has to be a minority strategy. If everyone walked around without a tie, my disregard for the convention wouldn't say much about me, one way or the other.

Counter-signaling has another implication: it is not always a good idea to disclose good news. When I received the contract to write this book, I hardly told anyone.

Paradoxically, reporting good news can make a person look bad. If we look anxious to reveal good news, our listeners assume that we don't come by good news very often. Or perhaps our listeners believe we consider the good news a stroke of marvelous luck. Did Michael Jordan need to tell his friends every time he scored thirty points in a game? A player on the verge of getting released or traded in the NBA might repeat this fact to his coach or general manager. Does Bill Gates go home at night and tell his wife he earned a lot of money that day? I doubt it.

When we have good news, we should often withhold it, at least if we can afford to wait (e.g., we won't be fired tomorrow). Sooner or later the news will come out anyway. If need be, let a supposedly disinterested third party carry the report. Our audiences and friends will marvel. "What a modest type he is!" and "I wonder what other good news he might be holding back. . . ."

Two economists, Rich Harbaugh and Theodore To, of Indiana University and the Bureau of Labor Statistics, respectively, ran a clever test of counter-signaling. They hypothesized that of all the people with a given title, such as Ph.D., the least successful people from that group should be the most likely to advertise that title. To check up on this hunch, the researchers looked at economics faculty at different institutions. Who uses titles such as "Dr." and "Professor" in voice-mail greetings and on course syllabi? Their study considered twenty-six different economics curricula, and counted the eight with doctoral programs as of higher status. The results do not surprise Mr. Tyler Cowen.

The authors, Harbaugh and To, tell us: "For voice-mail greetings, the use of a title is far less common at doctoral universities. Less than 4 percent of faculty use a title at doctoral universities while about 27 percent use a title at non-doctoral universities. A similar pattern holds in course syllabi. About 52 percent of faculty at doctoral universities use a title while more than 78 percent do so at non-doctoral universities."

An effective use of counter-signaling requires finesse. Most importantly, the counter-signaler must already hold some independent air of mystique. The best programmers show up for job interviews without ties. But their reputation usually precedes them to some degree. If a completely anonymous person shows up for an interview without a tie, the boss infers that he is a bum or just a random job candidate. But if the boss thinks the highly touted job candidate from Google might well be a genius—but isn't sure—the missing tie will add to the nerdy image.

This lesson is sad for those who hate managing what they signal. Counter-signals work only because their users have, at some point in the past, engaged in prior signaling. The mystique does not just fall from the sky, and the lesson is that we cannot avoid signaling.

Furthermore, effective counter-signaling must be subtle. When we counter-signal, we wish to avoid the appearance of consciously manipulating other people. To be seen as sending a counter-signal is not only gauche, but it reveals the person as not truly, fully, and completely established. The person is a poseur, pretending to reach for the highest levels of achievement, but in fact he is simply another bum who doesn't want to wear a tie.

Along these lines, the counter-signaler who is caught offends everyone. The truly established are offended by the pretense that the counter-signaler places himself among them. The ordinary Joes—who signal frantically with their ties—are offended that the counter-signaler thinks he is too good for their stupid little games. And other counter-signalers may worry that one of their kind has been outed. Did I mention that counter-signaling is risky?

Given these risks, who should engage in counter-signaling? I see a rough rule of thumb. If a profession has a great deal of upside potential but low downside risk, counter-signaling should be common. Tenured academics are a good example. The most famous earn fortune and fame, but the worst do not get fired. The best programmers land on their feet even if they are fired for long hair at one of their jobs.

When vocational risk is high on the downside and low on the upside, counter-signaling should be correspondingly rare. Most of the people who work as cashiers in Wal-Mart have no realistic chance of being promoted to top management. But if they mess up they will be fired without much hesitation. It is no surprise that they adhere to rigid codes about how to greet the customers, ring up sales, and report shoplifters. It is hard to imagine a Wal-Mart cashier rationally thinking: "I'll ring up sales my own way. That will show the people upstairs that I am top management material." But no, instead conformity rules.

Many of my friends believe that counter-signaling works better for men than for women. I agree. Perhaps our society still awards men more degrees of freedom, or it demands less from men in terms of physical appearance. Many potential counter-signals modify dress or physical appearance, and that means that women face harder and more competitive signaling problems. A man at work can just slap on a decent suit and tie, but a woman must choose and then maintain an entire image. The complexity of signaling might mean that life as a woman is more fun, more nuanced, and also more stressful, all at the same time.

6

The Dangerous and Necessary
Art of Self-Deception

DELUSION IS ONE secret to a good marriage. Your Inner Economist knows this, but it should also know that it is one of those insights that should not be bandied about at the dinner table.

If we spend enough time with a person, frustrations tend to build. Often we remember the slights and the unfairness more than the favors and kindnesses. Couples grow apart. Sixteen percent of married couples will admit to not having had sex within the last month, and I believe the real number is higher. Over time it becomes harder to keep a positive image of our spouses, yet it is essential that we do so.

To be more precise than this chapter's opening sentence, marital bliss is based on, among other things, selective forgetfulness. The couples who stay together are the delusional ones who look back on their pasts with rose-colored glasses. A good marriage requires knowing when to forget, and knowing when not to notice in the first place.

Psychologists have coined the phrase "marital aggrandizement" for an unrealistically positive assessment of one's spouse and marriage.

For instance, many couples, when given a questionnaire, will answer "My spouse doesn't make me angry," or "I do not recall arguments with my spouse." It was once thought only newlyweds could offer such answers, but couples who have been married for forty years or more will be equally positive. Those same people have a greater chance of lasting and happy marriages.

Happily married couples also tend to believe that they have more in common with their partners than they really do. They feel they are "kindred spirits" or "soul mates," even when, by more objective standards, that is not exactly the case.

Self-deception is not just for the married or betrothed. A survey of one million high school seniors recorded 70 percent as thinking they are above average in leadership ability; only 2 percent thought they were below average. When it comes to getting along with others, 60 percent of polled high school students thought they were in the top 10 percent of their peer group. Twenty-five percent of the students thought they were in the top 1 percent.

Most people think they are smarter than average, better drivers than average, and indeed simply "better people" than average. Few of us believe that our rivals and enemies have superior moralities or superior ways of life, even if we recognize that those people are more powerful or more successful.

If necessary, we will redefine the dimension of competition so we can win. No, I am not the best or the most frequently cited economist in the world, but I work on "the really important questions."

People talk down some of their skills in some areas to maintain a self-image of modesty. I do not think I am much of a bowler, and I admit gladly I cannot fix a broken computer. But I use these admissions to boost the identity I do have, and not to downgrade my final sense of moral worth. After all, a fully conceited person is sadly lacking in judgment and self-knowledge and that is not me. Don't get me wrong; even if I can't fix a computer, I know not to waste my time with hopeless projects.

It is particularly common for us to believe we are much improved over time. We condemn our previous selves as selfish, lacking in judgment, or simply less skilled. This artificial skepticism reaffirms that we are not simply boasting about our current virtues. Instead we seek to confirm the (usually false) impression that we are capable of taking a long, hard look at ourselves. Most of all, we wish to support our current and largely positive self-image. The past self is a sacrificial victim toward this end, just as our current selves will be criticized by our future selves ten or twenty years from now.

We think we are better judges of political truth than average and better judges of religious questions than average. Millions of Americans vote, even though about half of them are unlikely to improve upon the collective wisdom of the others. Not only that, many of us think—despite our protestations to the contrary—we are the best judges of political and religious truth *in the entire world.*

If we knew some better judge of truth, we would accept that person's opinions all the time and substitute them for our own. Few people are so deferential, even when confronted with differing views from others of clearly high IQ, education, expertise, or professional status.

Even the deferential think they are "the best spotters of people to whom we should defer" in the world. *No one understands politics better than my uncle.* When we cannot claim the credit ourselves, we seek the glory of affiliation.

On economic issues, few voters defer to the opinions of expert economists when it comes to technical questions such as the benefits of free trade. This reluctance to defer does not appear to be a well-grounded suspicion of experts. Many citizens are deliberately dismissive, stubborn, and irrational in their points of view. At the same time these people maintain a passionate self-righteousness. They are keener to talk

than to listen, the opposite of how "information-gatherers" would behave. Debates and exchange of information often polarize opinion rather
than producing agreement or even partial convergence.

People also tend to believe that their private self-interest coincides
with the national self-interest. They cannot fathom that their affiliated
causes are not always worthy.

The experts delude themselves too. Ninety-four percent of polled
university professors thought they were better than average at their
jobs, compared to their colleagues. A survey of sociologists asked each
professor how much influence he expected to achieve. Almost half of
the sample of 198 expected to become among the top ten leaders in at
least one of their specialties. More than half expected that others
would read their writings even after their careers had ended. This
same group could not identify most of the previous presidents of the
American Sociological Society, a relatively prestigious group of names.
Furthermore, there is no evidence from the study that expectations of
professional immortality become more realistic with age.

Self-deception occurs when people simply refuse to think about or
process information that they do not like. Similarly, people talk themselves into believing things that, at some level, they know to be dubi-
ous or downright false. This, strangely, is often okay.

But not always. Many Muslims, when confronted with decisive evidence of the role of Osama bin Laden in the events of 9/11, including
a taped boast of his role, responded by claiming that the evidence was
faked and that Osama was innocent. Some charged that the bombing
was a "Zionist conspiracy," masterminded by Israel. A Gallup poll
showed that 61 percent of the respondents, from nine Muslim countries, think Arabs had nothing to do with the attacks. Individuals often
stick with their political views even when a contrary reality stares them
in the face.

The proud need to self-deceive. How many of us would enjoy hearing a two-hour debate—Oxford style with formal rules—on the relative prominence of our virtues and flaws? Let's say—just to be generous—that the "virtue" side would win the debate. It might win hands down. Hearing the debate would still probably bring more pain than pleasure. If we wish to go through life as happy, productive people, fundamental doubts about how good we are need to be blocked from our conscious minds.

. . .

SELF-DECEPTION CAN BE our greatest friend or our worst enemy, as your Inner Economist has already divined.

Professional economists, who are used to thinking that people value information, or have "rational expectations," have begun to study self-deception only recently. Perhaps they have started spending less time with their mathematical models and more time thinking about how their students prepare, or rather do not prepare, for exams. In reality, how people perceive the world is one of the most important factors for understanding the operation of incentives. Whether we like it or not, people really do think it is "all about them." And that means we must take a close look at self-deception.

The concept of self-deception, in various forms, has a long history in Western thought. The Greeks, starting with Homer and Plato, were obsessed with the notion. Penelope doesn't really want Odysseus to come back home, nor is he truly so sad to be leaving again at the end of the story. Self-deception is a common motif in the plays of Shakespeare (a close reading reveals Romeo and Juliet to be quite unsure of their love) and also in the seventeenth-century French moralists, most notably La Rochefoucauld. Read his *Maxims*:

> We are so accustomed to disguising our true nature from others, that we end up disguising it from ourselves.

Or how about:

> No matter what discoveries we may have made in the land of
> SELF-ESTEEM many undiscovered territories still remain.

In the eighteenth century, Adam Smith described self-deception as
a central feature of human behavior. Freud stressed how the subconscious structures an individual's portrait of reality to fit his or her neuroses and biases. Sartre placed self-deception at the core of his theory
of the emotions; perhaps at some level he knew he was not intellectually honest in his endorsement of Stalin.

Let's go back to my favorite advice column, "Dear Prudie" on
Slate.com. A reader wrote, in part:

> After several years of searching for Mr. Right, I have met
> someone who holds great promise. . . . He is a soft-spoken man
> who treats me with great respect. He's been a widower for
> many years, raising his children alone and doing a marvelous
> job. He's a hard worker, honest, and seems very smitten with
> me. We have a great deal in common including our profession,
> which has been a real challenge for me since I have a
> nontraditional job in agriculture. The problem is, he's an awful
> kisser, something I find pretty important when it comes to
> intimacy.

My brutal view? She doesn't adore him as much as she thinks. Yes,
some basic technique is required, but kissing is 90 percent psychology
and connection. The woman needs to cut through the self-deception
and ask herself the honest questions. Why didn't she write to Prudie
"I love him"? Her sentences make him sound like a dullard whom she
will grow to despise.

Today, an entire sector of the American economy—gym
membership—appears based on self-deception. Most people overestimate how often they will visit the gym. They buy gym memberships

that make sense only if they are exercise hounds, and of course many of them are not.

A study of 7,752 gym members, spread across three health clubs and three years, confirms just how much we overestimate our propensity to exercise. Under one contract, the customer pays a flat monthly fee of more than $70. The people with this arrangement attend the gym about 4.3 times a month, on average. That works out to an average price per visit of slightly more than $17.

These same people could have bought a ten-visit pass, which would charge them exactly $10 per visit, a much lower price. The average expense would have been $43 rather than $70. (There was also a single-visit pass, for only $12, that would have been cheaper as well.) The average gym user, over the course of an entire membership, could save about $600 by opting for the ten-visit pass. A naive economist (as opposed to one's Inner Economist) might think that people will save the money, but that would be a mistake.

In reality, people spend more. They spend an average of $600 more. They spend because they are unwilling to confront their illusions about how much—or how little—they love exercise. Or they might think, incorrectly, that the flat fee will get them to go to the gym more often. Polls of these same users show that they expect to have enough visits to make the flat monthly fee worthwhile. Most of them turn out to be wrong.

Six hundred dollars. Think of it as the price of self-deception about exercise. Think of it as one measure of how strong an incentive we have to self-deceive, to think better of ourselves than we deserve.

This study produced another result. The people who don't visit the gym much take a long time to cancel their contracts. They don't like to admit they are lazy slugs. Gym attendance often slows to a trickle. But after the visits stop, an average of 2.31 months elapses before monthly members terminate their contracts. For 20 percent of the quitters, the cancellation lag is four months or longer. In any case, the average cost of non-immediate cancellation, following the last gym visit, runs $187. Did these people really think they would stick to it? We can add that sum to the costs of self-deception.

• • •

SUPPOSE WE WERE offered the option of surgery, or a pill, to correct our self-deception. This pill would eliminate all of our biased beliefs about ourselves. We would suddenly realize that we are (probably) no more moral than average, that our political beliefs are often stupid, and we didn't actually deserve that last promotion. All of our beliefs would be brought into line with the facts.

Don't take that pill.

Psychologists have written about "depressive realism." The depressed, even though their thought processes are often quite irrational, tend to have more accurate views about their real standing in the world. They are more likely to admit that in various fields of achievement they are no better than average, and they are more likely to realize that, in many regards, they are below average.

The depressed are typically self-deceived in one major regard—namely, they underestimate their likelihood of escaping depression. Many of the depressed expect to remain depressed forever. For the depressed, it feels as if the cloud will never lift, when in reality the condition tends to come and go.

It is a moot point whether depression causes a lack of self-deception, or whether a lack of self-deception causes depression. Probably cause and effect run in both directions. In any case we really do need our self-deception.

People who feel good about themselves, whether or not the facts merit this judgment, tend to achieve more. They have more self-confidence, they are more willing to take risks, and they have an easier time commanding the loyalty of others. Self-deception also protects against distraction. If individuals, as biological creatures, pursue a few major goals (e.g., food, status, and sex), self-deception may be an evolved defense mechanism against worries, distractions, and a loss of focus.

We get through life only because we continually ignore the fact that people are watching us, evaluating us, judging us, and, yes, condemning us. Imagine walking around, knowing every minute what other people were thinking about us. Most of us would find this unbearable rather quickly.

Imagine we all had Web sites that tracked our performance in life and our generosity toward others. There is an entire Web page devoted to monitoring the tipping habits of the famous. Tipping "saints" include Charles Barkley, Bill Clinton, and Robert de Niro. Less kind four-letter words are used for Al Gore, Tiger Woods, and O.J. Simpson. The waiter seems so friendly, but in fact he is judging us every minute:

> Recently, a pro-wrestler known as "The Rock" was a customer of mine at a well-known steak-house that has been in business for 50 years. He called ahead and asked for the restaurant to open early to accommodate him as he was trying to avoid fans. I got to be the lucky fool who had to pen and set-up for this joker. He ran with this little complaint, ten refills on his soda, too much butter on his garlic toast, etc. The whole ordeal was hardly worth the lousy $7.00 tip I got. While this did average to be about 25% [Your Inner Economist says, that's not bad!], I would think that a man that has dolls and watches in his likeness could have tossed at least a $20 for the extra time and service. This guy is not a "Rock" to me, just a cheap pebble.

Libel law prevents me from reproducing many of the other entries on this Web site. But just think, people talk and think about us—all the time—the exact same way that we talk and think about them. That is an uncomfortable prospect, no? Now put it out of mind and continue reading.

• • •

THE KEY TO doing well is to keep our self-deception as a general buffer, but to overcome it selectively for specific problems.

Small changes in incentives can make a big difference in our beliefs. For instance, UFO sightings are down dramatically in the last decade. Perhaps science-fiction movies are not as compelling as they used to be, but I think another factor is at work: cell phones and cellphone cameras.

"The spaceship was in a no-call dead zone? And you didn't snap a picture?"

"I'm sorry, honey. They immobilized my fingers with their secret ray guns."

The story is suddenly a little harder to swallow. Most of all, it is harder to fool oneself, not just one's spouse and friends. Researchers who have studied reported episodes of alien abduction have concluded that most of the believers are fully sincere.

We can make more mundane improvements. Many of us should drastically limit the number of errands we run. At the very least we should not let ourselves feel good about accomplishing errands. Often we let errands take up the day, if only to avoid facing more difficult problems, such as calling an angry client, finishing a dissertation, or fixing the roof. Errands are most dangerous when we self-deceive ourselves into feeling we are accomplishing something.

We are getting something done, it's just the wrong thing. Many children don't study hard for tests, so they can have an excuse if they don't do well. We put our egos on the line when we try hard. For this reason, parents don't always get better performance out of their children by increasing rewards and punishments for good and bad grades. The more there is on the line, the more the child feels pressured. The response is often self-sabotaging behavior to take off the psychological heat. The child adopts the self-deceiving mantra, "School isn't that important anyway." Raising rewards and punishments pushes the child into more self-deception, precisely when more self-reflection is needed instead.

As a general principle, trying to puncture people's delusions does not always make them better off. Often we switch into other, less-easy-to-refute but more harmful delusions.

In at least one way, life in the former Soviet Union was remarkably easy. If something went wrong, Soviet citizens always had something or somebody—other than themselves—to blame. The Communist Party really *was* at fault. Even chess players had this excuse, since it is believed that tournaments or matches were sometimes thrown to "party favorites." Of course the downside was that many Russians grew to accept or even welcome their political repression.

A capitalist economy, with its meritocratic pretensions, does not offer the same excuses for poor performance. When we fail under capitalism, we are led to think, rightly or wrongly, that we just weren't as good as our competitors. Self-deception does best when it complements our beneficial self-narratives.

Each day I stop writing just a bit before I have said everything I want to. I find it better to approach the next writing day "hungry" rather than "written out." That makes me feel like a person who loves writing and excels at it. Don't I love writing? After all, I always want to do more of it. Of course if I need this trick, perhaps my self-image as an ardent writer is not completely true; otherwise, why do I have to stop early? Nonetheless, this trick leads me to write more and also to love writing more.

When it comes to getting things done, the biggest enemy for most of us is a day spent not writing, not a day spent writing too little. If a person can write a page a day, that adds up to about a book a year, an enviable pace. So we writers need to invest in a self-image as people who get something done every day, and self-deception helps us achieve that.

Shopping is a critical time when we crowd unpleasant information—our budget—from our minds precisely when we most need it. Most people have "a looking mode" and "a buying mode." Once we shift into the buying mode, watch out. No matter how calm the person might appear, a kind of frenzy sets in. The parts of our brain are activated that register the prospect of reward and that downplay the possible risks to our finances. In the language of neuro-economics, our limbic systems place us in a "hot" mode. We literally cannot judge the costs of our spending, and we start looking for things to buy.

But the hot mode goes as quickly as it comes. We start with a fair degree of inertia, and, provided we are not pathological, we tend to slip back into that state. We need only break up our buying frenzy before it gets out of hand.

How might we apply the reins to our spending? Well, leaving our credit cards at home might be too risky. We do, after all, need to buy expensive items every now and then. I therefore offer two tips:

1. Make the first purchase a guilty pleasure, not a necessity, thereby causing initial remorse to set in. In other words, take the indulgence up front rather than tacking it on at the end.

   Often the danger comes when we buy big items—items we genuinely need—and tack on small frivolities without much thought. Okay, maybe we do need a new $800 suit jacket. But we should make the decisions about the discretionary ties and socks *first*, and not while we are walking to the counter with the jacket in hand.

2. Go to stores with multiple checkout counters and use them. We spend more when we can take all purchases to the same counter. Paying more than once breaks our momentum, and focuses our attention on costs and prices.

Yes, delusions keep us going, but sometimes we need more brutal self-testing, if only in small, segregated parts of our lives. When I teach Ph.D. macroeconomics, I run a simple experiment. I ask students to write practice exam questions for each other and post those on the Web, behind a link. The questions can be viewed at will, but until they start their practice exams the questions remain a secret.

The students are then supposed to practice these questions in their spare time. But too many people simply peruse the questions, ponder them, discuss them, and "feel" they have a handle on them. I tell the students to have a friend or spouse pick out five of the questions as a surprise. The student should write out answers, under simulated exam conditions, with the clock ticking.

The point is this: most people do not study very effectively. They study to feel they are trying. They study to feel better about themselves. They do not always study to succeed in their chosen field. They spend hours staring blankly at sheets of paper and nodding about what they understand. Students should spend more time trying to solve problems or answer questions, usually under simulated exam conditions and with a clock ticking. Tick, tick, tick . . . That's the way to go, and yes, the whole point is that it hurts.

Too few writers show around their early drafts. They don't want to hear it stinks. Often, the longer an author has labored on a draft, the less he wants feedback on the product. Secretly he fears that critical comments will drain his efforts. He tells himself the story "My draft is coming along fine. I am on the right track." This mantra gets him out of bed in the morning and in front of the computer. When he does ask for criticism, it is often too late.

I call it The Hammer. Most people are afraid of The Hammer. One key to success is to take doses of The Hammer when needed, yet without denting our (partially unjustified) optimism too much. When we fear The Hammer, we often try to hide behind other people.

That is one reason why we try to hide behind brainstorming sessions so often.

Brainstorming sessions are a counterproductive way of spending time. People usually think of more new ideas on their own than they do in a group. Psychologists refer to "the illusion of group productivity." One meta-study found that people were less productive in groups in eighteen of twenty-two comparisons. Furthermore, the larger the group, the greater the loss of productivity. We all know that many people rely too much on the work of others and become "free riders." Yet surprisingly, we still tend to think highly of group discussions. More than 80 percent of people polled think that group brainstorming produces better results than does individual brainstorming.

Self-deception is one culprit for this failure of perception. When we are in groups, someone else is usually talking. We feel less pressure. We don't feel stupid just because we are silent or devoid of new ideas. Rather the sense of continuous activity gives us the feeling of being engaged in collective discovery. If I am experiencing no revelation, well, maybe someone else is. After all, something good must be happening; why else would we all be gathered in this room? We do like being on teams, especially winning teams.

Many people, after working in groups, mistake other people's ideas for their own. After the meeting they feel better. Furthermore, if the problem is hard, everyone can see that everyone else found it hard, too; this makes us all feel better.

In contrast, when working alone, it is painfully obvious when no progress is forthcoming. The voice of your Inner Economist is not drowned out. You can't deny you aren't being productive, and you have no excuse.

Brainstorming groups perform the worst when group members are asked to wait their turn before speaking up. When people are waiting, they tend to rehearse their prepared speech in their minds. They oscillate between nervousness and imagining how they will stun the group with their brilliance. Most people will not start a search for new ideas. Many people, due to cognitive limitations, are *unable* to search for new ideas when they are waiting. The discussion becomes static.

In contrast to many brainstorming sessions, trying to compute probabilities is a useful means of generating self-knowledge. When we are truly in doubt about different career paths, or about marriage proposals, we should try to quantify the choices. We should sit down with a pen and paper and try to figure out what probability of which outcome would be required to make one choice better than the other.

This sounds impossibly wonky, but the goal is not to generate a rational number from the process. The claim is not that "expected utility theory" is somehow descriptively true or can reflect the complexity of our choices. The goal is to get people over their useless delusions. Thinking about numbers tends to slow down some of the least rational parts of our brains. It forces us to look at the matter from a less emotional perspective.

In this context, I view expected utility theory like going to a different cash register to ring up the purchase of socks. Most people, even the innumerate, could benefit by stepping back and reexamining their premises. Isn't that what business consultants do for us? Asking a fortune-teller might help as well, if only by allowing us to see whether we are pleased or distraught by what she predicts.

A highly intelligent and well-educated female friend of mine once mentioned that she and her former boyfriend were thinking of getting back together again. Or at least she thought they were thinking of this. "What do the betting markets say?" was my immediate and perhaps not totally polite response. I did not receive a straightforward or even a numerical answer.

I continued: "You know . . . what are the odds?"

"I don't know," she said.

"Of course you don't know. And I don't know who will win the next Super Bowl. That is what we have odds for. Because we don't know. So what are the odds? At what spread would you take one side of the bet rather than another? Surely your friends have been quoting you odds."

Believe it or not, they hadn't even considered quoting her odds.

"One in three," I said, "What do you think of that?"

I never got the odds, but from her reaction I believe we both knew what the likely outcome would be.

. . .

THE NEED FOR control, or feeling in control, is one of our greatest self-delusions. In the chapters where I described how to control the world I hope I made clear how important an experience of control is to human beings. In this chapter I hope readers see that it is possible to manage their own sense of control.

Why do so many people feel that driving is safer than flying, even though it is not? When we are driving we are steering the car. We feel that if something bad happens, we can respond and bring the car and its passengers to safety. That is misguided, but we like feeling in control.

We have a special fear of risks when we run the risk of bringing a catastrophe upon ourselves. Imagine the following frightful scenario.

A deadly influenza virus comes from Asia to our shores. There is no cure, and doctors estimate that a person's chance of dying a horrible and painful death from the virus is 10 percent. A vaccine is available, made from a weakened form of the virus. The vaccine cures most people, but kills 5 percent of them.

Clearly it is better to take the vaccine. A 5 percent chance of dying, however awful, is not as bad as a 10 percent chance of dying. Yet not everyone, when surveyed, wants to take the vaccine. Many people are more afraid of the risk they choose than the risk that might befall them.

A poll, published in the *Journal of General Internal Medicine*, indicated that only 48 percent of the responders said they would take the vaccine. The rest were too afraid of the danger they might bring upon themselves. True, this was only a questionnaire and perhaps many of these people would be more rational if they were on the verge of possible death or viral infection. But the mere fact that their intuitions pulled them away from the vaccine, in the questionnaire setting, shows that human beings do not approach these problems rationally.

Those same people were more likely to recommend the vaccine for others. They were especially likely to recommend the vaccine for people distant from themselves, such as strangers. Fifty-seven percent of the responders said they would give the vaccine to their children. Sixty-three percent said that, if they were doctors, they would give it to their patients. Seventy-three percent said that if they were directors of a hospital, they would give the vaccine to all of their patients.

It appears that people think more rationally about the choice when it does not concern themselves. The more personal the choice, the more likely that fear drives out reason.

When it comes to evaluating risks rationally, we also make mistakes at the level of national policy. Many policies for fighting an influenza pandemic focus on developing vaccines and quarantining the sick. Both methods reflect a mentality of control. The thought is: "If only we had the right vaccine, we could control the virus." Or: "If only we shut down travel, we can keep the virus in one place." But it is hard to develop the proper vaccine in advance, make enough doses quickly, and distribute the doses. Quarantines work for small islands, but they would probably fail for a highly mobile nation of 300 million people.

A different approach is to strengthen the response capabilities of our emergency rooms, in case of a pandemic. Many experts believe that this would be the best way to invest our limited resources. But of course that is a tough recommendation to swallow. It forces us to admit that perhaps we cannot control the virus. How many politicians like to say: "Yes, thousands or millions will die but we can save at least some of them." Even if true, that doesn't sound nearly as good as, "We will protect every American."

Our responses to terrorism show similar biases. We are reluctant to adopt policies that admit but minimize losses. Politicians are too keen to claim that the problem can be controlled. Sometimes spending more money on the local fire department is better than trying to track down and kill every would-be terrorist.

America typically responds to challenges by refusing to admit it can fail. We have a "can-do" mentality. We built the first atomic bomb, we put a man on the moon, and we revitalized the American economy in the 1980s and 1990s—all of which seemed just about impossible before we did it. This self-confidence is admirable and has been responsible for much American national greatness. Nonetheless, it also hinders American progress. We tend to seek out options that offer some chance, however unlikely, of invulnerability and supreme command. Instead we should sometimes admit that we cannot stop terrible events but we can make them somewhat less bad.

On a more personal level, a willingness to give up control can make us better teachers. When we teach our children how to drive, we like to pretend that they will never do anything stupid. We give them a lecture about the long list of things they should never do. We know they may not listen, but at least we go away feeling we did our best.

My approach is different. I taught Yana, my then-fifteen-year-old stepdaughter, how to drive. One day I started with: "The first thing we are going to do today is hit the curb. Drive over that curb, just not too fast." This is the best way to learn where the curb is. Yana is going to find the curb anyway, sooner or later, so let this learning occur under safe circumstances. And the next time she encounters the curb, it won't bring on any great panic.

"Nudge that cone, but gently."

"Put the car in park (the car has an automatic transmission) before you've brought it to a full stop." Everyone does that one anyway, so let her get it out of her system and learn the consequences in a safe way.

Similarly, we might also try making our children drive while you, the parent, are making funny noises, "acting mental" and screaming

"Billy Bob has a crush on Yana." At some point her friends will hand out the same treatment. Don't shy away from what the driving experience has in store for the child, no matter how unsettling it may feel.

Why don't most people teach these lessons? It is simple. We want to feel safe and lower our stress during and after the instruction. Who wants to remember that horrible feeling of the car jolting to a rapid halt while still in drive? In reality we should be less concerned with our own stress and more concerned with preparing the future driver for the real world. That means dealing with the possibility of error rather than denying it. It means managing your ability to deceive yourself; it means managing your sense of control.

• • •

JUST BECAUSE SELF-DECEPTION is necessary to live a happy life, it doesn't mean that self-deception is always good for broader society. To see how self-deception can backfire, take a fresh look at the art world. It's full of phonies. No, I don't just mean the people, I mean the artworks. Again, your Inner Economist already suspected this.

It's not just Rembrandts and Picassos painted in northern New Jersey. Many fields of art are full of fakes. In some areas, such as pre-Columbian art, there are possibly more fakes on the market than real items (and the real items are most likely stolen from legally protected archaeological sites, so arguably the fakes are the lesser crimes). Fakes of just about every famous painter—from Vermeer to Pollock—have been sold to informed and experienced buyers, and sometimes even verified by the experts.

Why might so many otherwise intelligent buyers be suckered? One reason is pride.

Most people who own a Picasso are very proud of their possession. The pride value of owning the artwork is often more important than the pleasure of looking at the piece. Many collectors go weeks without taking pleasure from what is on their walls. No matter how modestly we may behave when company visit, we are very much hoping they will notice the Picasso.

I would love to own a Picasso print from his "Vollard Suite" series. I would hang it downstairs in the living room, where *you* can see it, not upstairs in the bedroom where perhaps I would see it more. Some of these prints go for "as little as" $20,000 to $50,000, but many of my visitors would think they are worth millions or at least hundreds of thousands. Of course, it is rude to tell people the price that was actually paid.

This pride sounds like fun, and indeed it would feel wonderful to have it. But therein lies the danger. Many art customers and art owners do not want to look too closely at what they own, for fear of losing pride in their possessions. That "Dalí print" has been hanging above the fireplace for more than twenty years. It was a gift from dear old Dad, who bought it from a gentleman on a cruise ship. Dad was so proud to help hang that print over the fireplace. Poor Dad. Dear old Dad. If only he could see now how much that print is loved and admired. It always reminds us of Dad, who indeed was the most real guy you could imagine.

Suddenly you make a new friend and he just happens to work at Sotheby's. He also studied art history at Yale. The friend offers to bring the print in for inspection, or perhaps to research its provenance. But not everyone is keen to receive such assistance. After all, we think the print is real. It sure looks real, doesn't it?

Similar psychology operates when we buy a painting. We love that picture. We want to take it home. Our art dealer has made us feel special just by offering it to us. "Usually I offer a picture this good only to people who have been buying from me for years. But I know that you and your wife are building a very special collection."

Deep down, we realize that we don't actually know so much about art and the art world. Looking more closely won't reveal if the picture is real or not. It will just make us worry more. Imagine feeling so nervous for all those years to come, just because they could not trace one step in the picture's provenance. No documentation? Well, people lose silly pieces of paper all the time. I know that I do. So let's stop worrying. We have already decided that we can afford to spend the money. It sure looks real, doesn't it?

When many buyers behave this way, authenticity cannot be taken for granted. And given that the market operates as such, the first lesson is that not everyone should buy art.

The second lesson is that the more a buyer self-deceives, the more likely he or she should assemble a collection by bidding at Sotheby's or Christie's. Their curatorial staffs are not perfect, but they do work hard to protect the good name of the auction house. In contrast, while many private dealers are honest, they cannot detect fakes with equal proficiency. The auction houses, with their multimillion-dollar capitalization, are more scrupulous about fakes than just about any of the art dealers who serve us (well, unless you are one of my billionaire readers and have a very fancy art dealer . . .).

The typical item sold at Christie's or Sotheby's in New York is worth about $1,500. This price range is affordable for many of us. But going to the auction house is usually not as fun. Unless we are big spenders, no one comes up and holds our hand. No one tells us how important our collection is. No one tells us what a great price we are getting. The entire process is far more anonymous. The art has to market itself, unless of course we are big-name buyers.

Furthermore, we don't experience the thrill of *knowing* we can bring the picture home, or that we will receive delivery within two days. First one bids; novices and those who don't live in New York City probably bid by mail. Then the bidder must wait until the auction is held. All that time the bidder is wondering whether she bid too much or bid too little. It is not like eBay, where we can monitor other bids 24/7.

Winning the auction leads to doubts about overbidding, and later the so-called "buyer's remorse": "Why didn't anyone else think it was worth that much?" There is no dealer to talk us through the trauma of parting with the money. Not winning the auction leads to disappointment. The "ready to buy" circuits were excited in our brains, but we must start over again from scratch. We were so keen to get the art collection going, but alas we were thwarted.

These problems feel grim in the moment, but in reality they do not last for very long. The next auction season is not far away and, well, yes, patience is a virtue. In contrast, the costs of buying a fake are very high and very permanent. When we self-deceive, or chomp at the bit to get that new picture, we do not give those costs high enough weight.

True, buying at the auction houses is not for everybody. Many people need the immediate gratification of a take-home purchase to maintain their interest in art. Others collect in areas that are harder to fake (e.g., large, seventeenth-century Flemish wall tapestries). But most of us, if we wish to buy art, should pay more attention to what is sold in auction houses. It happens to be the next step toward becoming a cultural billionaire, at least once you have a working knowledge of what you actually like.

But this is not just a parable about art. It is actually a story about politics, and why we have so many "fakes" and "phonies" in public office. Once we have supported candidates for local or federal government, we are reluctant to turn against them. Often we are reluctant to look too closely in the first place. That's not you, of course—that is only how other people behave. The people you disagree with.

Of course it is often the things we feel best about in politics that are the source of the greatest self-deception. On MarginalRevolution.com, I once wrote some economic common sense:

> I would admit that we cannot take care of everyone and that we face tough trade-offs.

One reader wrote back:

NO. WE. DO. NOT. YES. WE. CAN.

Another reader wrote back:

Why can't we? Other industrialized countries do it [he was referring to national health insurance]. We'd have to raise taxes by
a nontrivial amount, to be sure, but we certainly could do it if
we wanted to.

But alas, no. We cannot.

Every day about 155,000 people die. They die in Europe too, even
in the social democracies. People die from heart attacks and they die
from the flu. Children drown in buckets and people die in car crashes.
We don't call these health-care problems, but they kill us nonetheless.
We could spend all of our money on health care and these people still
would die, sooner or later. Most would die sooner. We could repeal
"the Bush tax cuts" and they *still* would die. The world also has several
billion very poor people, and other billions of moderate but not wealthy
means. They count, too, and yes they are going to die as well, often at
tragically young ages.

We can take some limited group of these people and make them
better off by selective health interventions. We *should* do this. But we
should choose the targets of our benevolence carefully. No matter how
good a job we do, many more people will slip through our fingers. And
those who are "taken care of" receive only marginal improvements for
temporary periods.

Our natural tendency is to want to feel that we are taking care of
everybody. We will favor policies that give us this reassurance. In the
process we will often reject policies that take care of a greater number
of people.

Many people complain that America has more than forty-five million uninsured. Few people (other than research doctors) complain that the budget of the National Institutes of Health, which supports basic medical research, is not higher. Encouraging innovation—a long-term source of immense health gains—does not give us that same feeling of controlling immediate human suffering. In other words, because of self-deception we don't take enough care to address the real long-term problems, and sometimes we don't spend more money when we ought to.

• • •

FOR ALL OF its flaws, self-deception helps keep us virtuous. Most good things we do—and I include charity—we do not do for the ends themselves, but because we have somehow learned to enjoy the process of regular engagement and self-discipline. We then deceive ourselves into thinking we value the end—be it exercise, charity, or whatever—more than we do. We think that we are better people than we really are, but to some extent this trickery is a self-fulfilling prophecy. If we can talk ourselves into acting and thinking like truly and deeply benevolent people, so much the better.

When we think our work is important, we are happier and we do a better job. Perhaps our individual efforts really aren't significant in the broader scheme of things. But if presidents, prime ministers, and popes were the only individuals who felt "they mattered," our world would collapse. Similarly, if we are to expect the full energies and brilliance of our artists, they need to believe that their creative works are of earth-shattering social and aesthetic importance. The fiction of a truly objective person would probably be a robot with no emotions and real sense of self—who would want that, either for herself or for others?

Nonetheless we should all strive to become, at the margin, less deluded on critical issues, while retaining our enthusiasm for life. If we can improve our perception of reality, the wisdom of the world lies literally at our fingertips.

Often we don't ask what we are doing wrong when we date, dress, or deal with our friends, spouses, and children. We are afraid of what the honesty of others will do to our feelings and what it will do to our motivation.

We need to invest in a different self-image and different narratives. Instead of repeating "My draft is coming along fine," or "I already know how to dress," try "I am the best person in the world at listening to advice." Few of us are very good at taking advice, but this tale will make us just a bit more receptive. We will be able to learn and achieve in new and powerful ways.

7

Eat Well, Bananas Aside

FOOD IS THE most universal sensual pleasure, and of course it is our required sustenance. Braised sweetbreads, oyster casserole with ginger and scallions, and stewed collard greens are there for the taking, if only we have the money and the knowledge. Unlike with art museums, it is not hard to get ourselves to pay attention to good food. The main problem is finding, evaluating, and possibly creating culinary treasures.

A few simple rules, taken from our Inner Economist and from an understanding of incentives, can help us eat much better meals. Books on food are legion, but few deal with the profit and loss behind making and selling food. Yet food is a market product, and it is the result of capitalist supply and demand. If we understand the economic laws governing dining, we can find better food, and often we can find excellent food at reasonable prices.

I'll talk about home cooking later in this chapter, but let's start with restaurants. You might remember that our first look at incentives started with whether or not you can pay your daughter to do the dishes. We learned *you can't buy everything*. Well, the trick to using home cooking properly is to figure out what you can't buy anywhere else, or what is especially cheap or tasty to make at home. So we can't understand either restaurants or home cooking without keeping our eye on this broader picture of how the two should fit together.

• • •

THE WORLD OF restaurants is not always easy to navigate. A well-developed metropolitan area will have hundreds of different dining locales. I've written about restaurants near my home in northern Virginia for years. While my "Ethnic Dining Guide," as I call it, is far from complete, my reviews still fill more than one hundred pages of single-spaced text. Of course each place has its own menu, and especially with ethnic cuisines we often do not know what to order.

Despite the amazing plenitude of food choices before us, we need not feel completely lost. We just need some simple principles for narrowing down what to order, which restaurants to visit, and which cities to visit. Let us start with the menu and then work back toward the more fundamental choices of location.

At fancy and expensive restaurants ($50 and up for a dinner is an imperfect benchmark for this category), there is a simple procedure. Look at the menu and ask yourself: "Which of these items am I least likely to want to order?" Or, "Which of these sounds the least appetizing"? Then order that item.

The logic is simple. At a fancy restaurant the menu is well thought out. The time and attention of the kitchen are scarce. An item won't be on the menu unless there is a good reason for its presence. If it sounds bad, it probably tastes especially good.

When I hear "monkfish" usually I think of a thick, fleshy fish, easily prone to abuse and overcooking. It is very hard to make good monkfish. Most people, and most restaurants, shouldn't even try. I don't try.

But when the monkfish is paraded with pride on the menu of a very good restaurant, it is usually an excellent entrée. The dense and sweet flesh does very well in the hands of an expert chef. Other difficult-sounding but usually high-quality items at good restaurants include game (easy to overcook, and hard to procure fresh), anything you have never heard of, and most of all organ meats, especially the nasty-sounding ones.

Many popular-sounding items can be just slightly below the menu's average quality. Beware roast chicken. The problem, in fact, is that roast chicken is too often okay. I can cook reasonably good (and sometimes excellent) roast chicken. Many "dining wimps" will order roast chicken to experience the familiar. Roast chicken can end up on a menu of a good restaurant even when its preparation is not superlative. Fried calamari is usually tasty at fine restaurants, but rarely do crispy items exceed a certain level of interest. As with roast chicken, too many people love fried calamari, so it will be on many menus no matter what. Its general popularity suffices, but it doesn't hit the highest peaks of taste.

In plain language: order the ugly and order the unknown. In a fancy restaurant, order the item you are least likely to think you want.

There is one caveat for this rule. Don't take these chances if your taste is no better than that of the less "food sophisticated" diners at fancy restaurants. Maybe roast chicken is all you can stand. Yes, that describes some people, but many of us can move to more interesting and varied diets; we simply need that extra push to try something new and unusual.

There is a flip side to this advice: when cooking at home, be wary of trying something new. Start by eating that same dish at a good restaurant. The restaurant menu is preselected by an expert and fine-tuned by other tasters and of course the other diners. That process, however imperfect, probably embodies more wisdom than your random hand in the kitchen. Your dining and your cooking knowledge often complement each other, but when it comes to new dishes you should usually start with the dining, and the cooking can follow.

Here is another strategy in fine restaurants: ask the waiter what should be ordered. It is important, however, to phrase the question properly. Think about the waiter's incentives. Even at temples of haute cuisine, a waiter might have instructions to push a high-margin item or to market a standard dish that the kitchen has prepared in large numbers that evening. Don't just ask the waiter "What should I get?" The waiter may try to get rid of you quickly so as to move on to his next task. The waiter may also think you are no smarter, in culinary terms, than the average diner. Even at a good restaurant this can be an insulting assessment.

I prefer a more pointed question. I ask the waiter "What is best?" I am happiest when the waiter does not hesitate to tell me what is best. "The rare tuna in the ginger sauce is best, sir" is the kind of answer that warms my heart. I order it. Conversely, I get nervous when the waiter responds: "All of our menu items are good." Even worse is: "Best? That depends on your point of view. Our customers enjoy many different items." Also bad is a nervous smile, followed by, "What do you mean by 'best'?" All of these latter responses are signs of cowardly waiters who are not used to dealing with demanding foodies. Remember the chapter on how to look good? These waiters are signaling that they have never been given exacting instructions by a quality boss or chef.

If asked, "What do you mean by best?" I simply respond, "Best. I am a Platonist. [This, of course, refers to Plato's theories of the forms, as expressed in the dialogue *The Republic*, which explains the idea of an absolute, perfect truth, as might be found in the heavens.] Best, as in 'Best.' I want The Best."

If that kind of philosophical talk doesn't suit your style, it is worth referring to the restaurant's "signature dishes." Or mention being a serious foodie who travels long distances to find wonderful meals. If a straight answer still is not forthcoming, well, you haven't ordered yet. It is time to pay the bill for the drinks and head elsewhere.

Of course when you are cooking, unless you are a true expert, it is often best to reverse this advice. Don't try to cook the signature dishes of your favorite restaurant. Maybe it is a fun challenge, and if so go ahead, but it is not the best way to eat. Those dishes are probably, by design, difficult to reproduce, if only to ensure the competitive advantage of the chef. It is still the case that your roast chicken can taste very, very good.

At ethnic restaurants, many of these problems are harder to deal with. Many Chinese waiters and waitresses simply refuse to recommend their best dishes to Western-looking customers. Begging and pleading for "real Chinese food" might not bring anything better than Kung Pao Shrimp. Asking for "what is best" will probably ensure chicken with broccoli, not the chicken kidneys in XO sauce (XO sauce is made with chopped, dried seafoods, fried in onion, garlic, chili, and oil), or the more modest scallion fried fish. Many Chinese waiters and waitresses still express marvel that a Western diner can eat with chopsticks at all.

Often the best option is to point at what other people are eating. "Bring me what they have" will work, and perhaps the menu doesn't make much sense anyway. Or perhaps it is possible to speak with helpful Chinese diners at a nearby table. But what if the restaurant is empty, or none of the other diners appear to be qualified (or some appear *too* qualified, and we just don't want the fried duck blood tonight)?

We still have a means forward. Before going to the restaurant, we should do just a tiny bit of research. We should memorize the name of one "second-tier" city in the relevant country or region. At a Sichuan restaurant, say confidently to the waiter "I know Chengdu. (Pause) Bring me the food of Chengdu. I love Chengdu." This does not involve a lie, as the word "know" is vague; it might, for instance, mean "to possess information about."

This geographic claim signals at least a small amount of expertise about the cuisine. Chengdu has about ten million people, and it is a center for Sichuan dining, but alas, few Americans know Chengdu. Last I read, only about 10 percent of the young American population could locate Afghanistan on a map of Asia. So mentioning Chengdu to a Chinese waiter will make you stand out. The reference will elicit a mix of sympathy, curiosity, and support. The waiter might just recommend the delicious Sichuan chili chicken. He will no longer think that you, a Westerner, will be put off by the glistening coat of red chili peppers on top of the dish. But don't worry, not too much of the spiciness soaks into the underlying bits of chicken.

If you are in a Cantonese restaurant, with lots of seafood, try mentioning Shenzen. Barbecued goose and shark fin are both local specialties, but it doesn't matter whether you want these dishes. You have shown the waiter that you are serious. You have sent the appropriate signal.

Sometimes these signals are not enough. Send all the messages you want, but the restaurant isn't there just for you. Other people have to foot the bill too, and we all know that few Americans have heard of Shenzen. Sometimes the stuff we want simply isn't available. Where I live, near Washington, D.C., I can't find barbecued goose at all. That's where cooking reenters the picture, and yes that dish is wonderful for Thanksgiving.

If you are in an ethnic restaurant in the United States, and the waiters and waitresses are simply not helpful, here is some general advice for how to think about the menu:

1. Avoid dishes that rely too heavily on top-quality raw ingredients. Unless we are somewhere fancy and expensive, American raw ingredients—vegetables, butter, bread, meats, etc.—are based on mass production and thus they are below world standards. Even most underdeveloped countries have better raw ingredients than

does the United States. Ordering the plain steak in Uruguay or Bolivia may be a great idea, but it is usually a mistake in northern Virginia. Opt for dishes with interesting sauces and complex mixes of ingredients. Bet on the ability of the chef to come up with a good idea and execute it well.

In a Bolivian restaurant, this might mean asking for the silpancho, a specialty of the Cochabamba region. Yes there is a plain steak underneath, but underneath that are rice and potatoes, and piled on top are scrambled egg, tomatoes, onions, and green chili sauce. To be blunt, the steak just does not have to be that good for the overall meal to be delicious.

Depending on the supermarket you use, or the farms you have access to, you might want to consider a similar rule for your cooking.

2. Appetizers are often better than main courses.

Just like not every gag can be turned into a good movie, not every good dining idea can be sustained for a full-sized plate of food. The value of the initial taste surprise may not sustain more than a few bites. For that reason, meals composed of appetizers and side dishes can be very satisfying.

Thai and Lebanese restaurants are especially good at presenting interesting small dishes, salads, and appetizers. In a Thai restaurant try a spicy pork salad with peanuts (*nam sod*), a chicken satay, *mee krob* (sweet noodles with tamarind sauce), and the soups with coconut milk. Don't just get a plate full of curry or noodles, familiar though it may be.

3. Avoid desserts.

Most ethnic restaurants in America, no matter how good, usually fall flat with the desserts. Especially if the restaurant is Asian. Calcutta has some of the world's best sweets, but it takes a lot of time and trouble to make them right and to ensure that the ingredients are fully fresh. Quality Indian sweets are usually profitable only when the cost of labor is very low, and that is not the case in either Chicago or London.

Also keep in mind that in many parts of the world, refined sugar was a novelty until recently. If a person hardly ever consumes refined sugar, even a simple dessert like a sugary bean paste will taste wonderful. To a palate spoiled by sugar, as is usually the case in the developed West, that same bean paste is a disappointment. So, Calcutta aside, many of the very best desserts tend to be found in regions that have had refined sugar in the diet for a long time. Start with France, Germany, Switzerland, and Austria. China had been poor a long time, so most of its desserts won't appeal to diners in the richer parts of the world.

4. Order more dishes than you plan to eat.

We don't eat out every night, so we are ordering for variety, and for new experiences, not just to fill up. We can always take the rest home.

Many cuisines are meant to be eaten by large numbers of people—usually extended families—around a common table at the same time. Dishes are created and selected for their variety and for their role in a broader meal plan. Historically, if a country has had a high population and a high birth rate, the cuisine has evolved in such a way that multiple courses create the best meal.

If a group of three people is visiting a good Chinese restaurant, the group should order at least five dishes. Yes it costs more, but make up the difference by cooking more at home or skimping somewhere else; don't waste a visit to a tasty restaurant. The best Chinese food is meant to be eaten in a sequence of courses, balancing difference flavors, temperatures, and textures. A smoothly textured soup will set the groundwork for a "salt and pepper shrimp," a dish with chili, and then a sweet-and-sour sauce. Ordering one dish is like hearing one movement of Beethoven. We are left wanting more, and at least some Inner Economists are prone to being more disappointed than if they had never shown up in the first place.

• • •

SO MUCH FOR quick tips once inside the restaurant. How do we find the right restaurant in the first place? Where in a city should we look? In what kinds of cities, or countries, should we expect to find good food?

Let us say we are in a strange city, or a strange country, and we want to try something other than the native cuisine. We want to try that country's "ethnic food." The best advice is to patronize the cuisine that is represented by the greatest number of restaurants. The restaurants are competing against each other, they are drawing upon a common pool of workers, and they draw upon a network of expertise for that cuisine. The city or region will have a great deal of local knowledge about how to make that cuisine work, given the raw ingredients at hand. In other words, competition works.

Here is a table of advice for eating ethnic food abroad:

Country	Restaurants
France	Algerian or Tunisian.
Germany	Turkish, Greek, or any of the Balkan cuisines.
England	Pakistani and Indian food; cooked in the U.K. these are still better than most British cuisine.
Netherlands	Indonesian or Surinamese (both formerly Dutch colonies)

(*continued*)

Country	Restaurants
Canada	Chinese (especially in Vancouver), Caribbean, and Eastern European cuisines, such as Hungarian or Ukrainian.
Argentina	Italian; these are wonderful almost everywhere in South America, but especially in Argentina and southern Brazil, both of which are full of Italian immigrants.
Mexico	Argentinean steakhouses.
Dubai	Indian, Pakistani, and Persian. Dubai is near the Persian Gulf, but most people living in the city-state are guest workers from the Indian subcontinent; Dubai has even been called the best-functioning Indian city.

For those looking to take a food vacation, I have a recommendation. Choose a country with a great deal of inequality. It sounds heartless, but look for a big gap between the rich and the poor. Iron bars on the windows and barbed wire on the fences, however bad for the residents or for your safety, are both good signs for the food.

The presence of a wealthy class of people, all other things equal, is good for food because the wealthy are a strong market for a tasty meal. That encourages quality food.

But when we look at producers, a certain amount of poverty is, sad to say, likely to produce gourmet meals. The higher the level of wages at the bottom, the harder it is to employ labor to cook the food, prepare the raw ingredients, and serve and bus the tables. So the committed foodie should look to regions where some people are very rich and others are very poor. The poor people will end up cooking for the rich people. My meals in Mexico, India, and Brazil are typically delicious and cheap.

Haiti, despite being the poorest country in the Western hemisphere, has some of the best food in the Caribbean. Per capita income is about $400 per year. Life expectancy is about fifty years, and most Haitians live in shacks. An upscale Haitian restaurant in the relatively wealthy suburb of Petitionville will hire many laborers for each diner. The mushrooms are picked and carried in by hand. The pork, the fish, and the vegetables are all produced and cooked with great personal attention. The service is extremely good and attentive.

There are few ways to earn good money in Haiti, so if foreigners and U.N. monitors are visiting restaurants, Haitians will work there. I once asked a Port-au-Prince cabbie whether he thought the U.N. troops were good for his country. "Very good for the people who sell lobster" was his response.

High wages are one reason why Western Europe is losing its historic role as culinary leader. Parisian restaurants must pay high wages, high benefits, and face tough labor laws. That is why so many top Parisian restaurants are closed on both Saturday and, almost certainly, Sunday. In the United States such hours would be unthinkable. Even though the United States has a high average level of wages, the country has more immigrants, more part-time labor, and a greater dispersion of wages. It is much easier to find low-wage labor in the United States and much easier for people to work long hours without breaking the law.

The Anglo-American nations, such as the United States, Canada, U.K., Australia, and New Zealand, all have relatively free labor markets and relatively liberal immigration policies. Thirty or forty years ago, these countries were culinary losers, famous for their bland meats and their boiled vegetables. Today they are all up-and-coming hotspots, gaining on the older culinary reputation of France. Many restaurants—whether haute cuisine or ethnic dining—in the Anglo-American world are staffed and run by immigrants. Few of those workers expect six weeks' vacation or a sharply limited work week.

It is not unusual for a French chef to move to New York, to hire Mexicans to cook French food for an American clientele, or perhaps to cook for French tourists visiting New York City. The key element in this equation is the Mexicans and their freedom to sell their labor. The Mexicans are the reason why the French chef is serving French food to French tourists near Lincoln Center, rather than in Lyon.

In the United States most of the French food—arguably most of the *food*—is cooked by Mexicans, not by Frenchmen. Frenchmen cost too much, but millions of Mexicans, in their home country, still earn only a dollar or two a day. Many of them would rather cook in the United States for ten to twenty dollars an hour, even if it means cassoulet rather than *carne asada*.

In India the very poor cook for the wealthy, perhaps in restaurants but more commonly as their servants. It has been said that India consists of two nations. About 100 million people have living standards comparable to those of Europe, and about 900 million people live in poverty, often on a dollar or two a day. The 100 million are all hiring domestic cooks, and the 900 million are competing for the jobs of serving the food and doing the household chores.

The Nordic countries, of which I am fond, have much more income equality. Hardly anyone in Norway is poor or even lower middle class. This may be to the credit of Norway, but it does not help their food. The more equal the distribution of income, the more it costs to hire kitchen labor. The Nordic countries look to ethnic foods cooked by immigrants. In Stockholm it is often easier to find good Indian food, or for that matter good pizza, than to find good Swedish food, especially once we take price into account.

Again, this also implies some tips for what you should cook at home. You should cook at home what you can't find in restaurants. If you live in rural Alaska, perhaps you should use mail order to get those ancho chiles and perfect your skills at Mexican food. But say you live in Los Angeles or New York, two cities that have just about every kind of ethnic food? What should you cook? The answer is simple: you should learn German food, Scandinavian food, and other foods from egalitarian countries with high wages. Those will be the hardest to find in good local restaurants, for precisely the reasons explained above. If there is a good German restaurant in Los Angeles, chances are that Mexicans are doing the cooking.

After thinking about wages, our Inner Economist, in search of better food, should turn his or her attention to rent. Restaurants must pay rent each month, no matter how many customers walk through the door. For that reason, the level of rent constrains what kind of restaurant can survive in a given locale. A little bit of knowledge about rent helps us find that wonderful mom-and-pop ethnic restaurant.

High-rent activities include chain clothing stores, Starbucks, the Disney Shop, and Tiffany & Co. An upscale mall is full of high-rent stores. A high-rent store typically attracts a large number of paying customers per hour, charges high markups on its goods, or both. Low-rent activities include dollar stores, antique and secondhand shops, and the Chinese restaurant in a suburban strip mall. The trappings are ordinary rather than glamorous.

When rent is high, restaurants will either be for the masses, or they will be very expensive. Midtown Manhattan is full of wonderful eateries, but the best ones cost $300 to $400 per dinner, not including wine. These restaurants are near the homes of millionaires and billionaires, and near the central tourist, theater, and shopping areas of Manhattan. Alternatively, some fine restaurants opt for lower rent and locate near the vacation spots of the wealthy.

While most fine restaurants are in high-rent areas, most restaurants in high-rent areas are far from fine. Manhattan and other large cities are full of T.G.I. Fridays, Sbarros, and Hard Rock Cafes. These locales provide bland, predictable food and weak beer. They stay in business by generating volume, usually by appealing to the lowest common denominator.

One good way to find a tasty and cheap meal is to seek out low-rent areas near higher-rent customers. In Los Angeles, eat Mexican food in East Los Angeles or Asian food in Koreatown. There are better food buys in East Hollywood than West Hollywood, where the movie stars live. Good, cheap ethnic food in Manhattan has been pushed away from the center of town; we can do better on Ninth Avenue (the far West Side), or First Avenue (the far East Side), than on Fifth Avenue or Broadway. Queens and Brooklyn have better and more varied ethnic food than does Park Avenue. If you must try Park Avenue, start below 35th Street, and look for cheaper apartments. If you wish to find the undiscovered mom-and-pop restaurant, the real-estate listings are often more useful than a *Zagat* dining guide.

Manhattan avenues tend to be higher-rent than locations on the cross-streets. Given the long, thin shape of the island, the north-south avenues carry more vehicular and foot traffic. A Fifth Avenue spot will be seen by most city residents and visitors at some point or another. A storefront on 39th Street will be seen mostly by neighborhood locals. Only a few broad cross-streets, such as 86th or 57th or 14th, take on the economic properties of the up-and-down avenues. If you are stuck in midtown, and you want good, cheap ethnic food, try the streets before the avenues. That neat Korean place can make ends meet on 35th Street but would not survive on Fifth Avenue. In other words, no matter where you are, turning just a bit off the main drag can yield a much better meal for the money.

Taking this logic one step further, we should dine in suburban strip malls, at least if the relevant suburbs have lots of recent immigrants. Most ethnic restaurants in the United States seek low-rent locations. Chinatowns were long ideal for this purpose, but the suburban strip mall has become more important as an outlet for ethnic diversity. It is common to see good ethnic restaurants grouped with mid-level or junky retail. My favorite Chinese restaurant in Virginia is next to a Kinko's, a nail parlor, a Marshalls (low-price clothing and furniture), a shop for selling school uniforms, and a store for remaindered Japanese kitchen items and plasticware.

Low-rent food venues can experiment at little risk. If a food idea does not work out, the proprietor is not left with an expensive building, fancy decor, or a long-term lease. A strip mall restaurant is more likely to try daring ideas than is a restaurant in a large shopping mall. The shopping mall restaurant pays a higher rent, and has invested more in decor. It will try to attract a large number of customers, which usually means predictable, mainstream food, the scourge of the dining sophisticate.

If I am in a hitherto unknown part of the United States, the region has immigrants, and I am looking to eat, I head away from the center of town. I look for the strip malls. The best strip malls, for food, are those without Wal-Mart, Best Buy, or other "big box" stores. Large anchor stores encourage high rents and large crowds, which are not always the right combination for interesting ethnic food.

Lower rents also mean that more people can try their hand at starting a restaurant. Many more people can try to market the family cooking. Few immigrant families can afford to rent or buy a restaurant space in the middle of downtown Philadelphia, or for that matter in the middle of an upper-middle-class shopping center, such as Tysons Corner (northern Virginia), South Coast Plaza (Orange County), or Paramus Park (northern New Jersey). The people with the best cooking ideas are not always the people with the most money.

The key to understanding the current evolution of dining in the United States is that rents are rising. The expensive places are costing more and more. The ethnic foods found in the middle of high-rent cities are becoming more upscale. The cheap, experimental, and low-decor ethnic foods are moving to the geographic fringes. The same is happening in London, Paris, Berlin, and even Mexico City, among other major urban areas. And just as high rents push out quirky food, so do they push out quirky culture, including clubbing scenes and offbeat art galleries. In New York both ethnic food and experimental music are moving to Brooklyn and Queens, largely because of high rents in Manhattan. Gentrification is good for the neighborhood, but it is not always a blessing for culture.

We can again work backward and draw some inferences about what you should cook at home. If you live and work in high-rent districts, perfect your hand at funky Chinese and Mexican, and I don't mean beef with broccoli or tacos. Opt for Sichuan hot pot and exotic pumpkin seed moles. If you live in a dump, and don't like to drive long distances, figure out how to sear foie gras.

The culinary advantages of low rents help explain why street food and food stalls are so often so good around the world.

Food stalls, as found in Asia, Mexico, and many other parts of the developing world, are low-rent venues in the extreme. They typically bring together many small "kitchens" under a common roof. In Mexico a single food stall takes up enough room for a few people to stand and a few tables. The central market of a city might have twenty to a hundred such food stalls, or *comedores*, as they are called in Spanish. The customer can buy Grandma's cooking, and true regional cuisine, for no more than a dollar or two.

Sadly, food stalls do not always survive urban development; they're generally a low-rent rather than high-rent activity. As city land becomes more valuable, especially in the center, food stalls and food markets are moved outside the city center. Even in Oaxaca, a Mexican dining capital, the best stalls are now outside the city center. In city centers, more formal cafeterias and restaurants have taken over the customers formerly served by the stalls. The newer venues offer greater selection, and finer eating quarters, but the food is usually blander and less fresh.

Food in Singapore is so good because the city has harnessed the magic of food stalls. Chinese, Indians, and Malays have long loved quality food. The general wealth of the city allows people to eat out a lot, while land-use policies have ensured that food stalls are not pushed out by higher rents.

Collections of food stalls—or "hawker centers," as they are called—are found throughout the city. In virtually any part of town the stalls will sell an excellent meal for $2 or less. Given that Singapore is as wealthy as France, this price is astonishing, especially since Singapore serves some of the best Chinese, Indian, and Malay dishes in the world. Singaporean cognoscenti insist that the very best Singaporean food is found in the stalls and not in the restaurants.

A contemporary hawker center is typically found outside the center of downtown, usually under a large metal roof. It might contain fifty or more food stalls, usually of Chinese, Malay, and Indian cuisines. The Chinese food in particular is quintessentially Singaporean, and it does not correspond to what might be found in China; in the hawker centers Chinese cooking has borrowed and incorporated Indian and Malay ideas. For instance, fish-head curry, which is original to Singapore, draws its curry sauce from South India but the idea of the fish head is Chinese; Indians would use fish fillet. Singaporean crab, one of the country's classic dishes, combines Chinese (bean paste), Malay (chilis), Indian (sauce texture), and Western (tomato sauce) influences.

Most stalls specialize in a small number of dishes, and often the stall builds its reputation on a single dish, or a single dish with close variants. So there will be *nasi goreng* (fried rice with egg), rice porridge, *roti john* (a kind of meat loaf with chili sauce), and grilled stingray.

The best cooks spend several years working on their own, perfecting their specialty dish, before taking it public in a hawker center. The owner is usually on site, cooking or at least overseeing the food. Since many different kinds of stalls are right nearby, a single stall can specialize in two or three key dishes. Customers buy their fried oyster egg from one expert and their *laksa* (noodle soup, in coconut milk) from another expert. This specialization, combined with tight monitoring of quality, is another reason why Singaporean food is so delicious.

But make sure you have enough time to eat. The stalls cannot easily scale up the volume of food when demand is high, so customers have to wait in long lines. For many of the most popular dishes, the wait can take over half an hour.

Until the 1960s, street hawkers were a common sight around Singapore. Usually there was no table and the customer had to eat standing up or take the food home. Sometimes the hawker would wander by on foot, carrying the food on a pole on his shoulders; other early hawkers used tricycles. Gradually the hawkers gathered in common centers, such as Colombo Court, Bugis Street, Hokkien Street, Beach Road, and so on. Ten or twenty hawkers might gather in each locale. Over time, a locale would become known for a particular kind of food; Hokkien Street, for instance, was known for its Hokkien Mee, a kind of fried noodle.

In the 1960s the Singaporean government tried to eliminate the food stalls, which were viewed as unsanitary and chaotic. But slowly policies changed. By the 1970s, the government was willing to organize regular hawker centers, complete with electricity and sanitation. In part hawker centers were seen as drawing people to nearby public housing. It is also rumored that authorities felt that quick and easy eating would make the population work longer hours, rather than rushing home to cook. Some Singaporeans do not keep a kitchen, but rather rely on food stalls and hawker centers for their sustenance. Later it was realized that the hawker centers attracted tourists.

The political momentum has continued to favor the stalls, which now are seen as a kind of public utility or public right. The technocratic Singaporean government reserves land for food stalls throughout the city. Rents may rise, but it is not easy to buy out the stalls and set up a large shopping center on the same ground.

I might add that the hawker stalls are exceptionally clean. The Singaporean government sends around a food inspector who gives a letter grade to each stall. Everyone in Singapore knows it is safe to eat in the stalls; customers can see the kitchen and the cooking. Most of the stalls receive a "B" grade from the inspector. The standing joke is that the stalls with grades "C" or lower have the tastiest food, and that an "A" grade represents too much attention to cleanliness and not enough time spent on the food.

In addition to the hawker centers, Singapore has food courts in shopping malls. These venues have a more upscale feel than the stalls and they are usually air-conditioned. The food tends to be blander, higher-priced, and it is made by a rotating variety of part-time employees, rather than by a single master of the craft. The menu is longer, but no one dish is as good as in the stalls. Customers are paying for the comfort, the air-conditioning, and the relative lack of lines. If you truly wish to be a culinary billionaire, the hawker centers are the place to go.

• • •

IF FOOD STALLS are an example of successful low-rent food, Las Vegas dining has managed to prosper as rents have risen rapidly. The city has a special advantage: it attracts gamblers, many of whom are very wealthy and looking for a good meal on vacation. Yes, the tastes are wonderful, but our Inner Economist tells us that Las Vegas—unlike Singapore—is no longer such a food bargain.

Up through the 1980s, casinos offered visitors luscious buffets with lobster, steak, and shrimp. The classic buffet at the Circus Circus casino charged only $1.90 for dinner (and $1.25 for lunch) in the 1970s. Lines stretched out the door and many of the visitors stayed to gamble, thus financing the entire venture. The theory was that food brought in gamblers. Why eat in one casino and walk to another when it's a hundred degrees outside?

In essence, the winnings from the casino subsidized the restaurants. The casinos made money on the gambling, so they used the food to lure visitors, which meant high quality and low prices. The earlier Las Vegas was the classic example of what economists call a cross-subsidy. One service—in this case gambling—cross-subsidized the production of another service, namely good food. The presence of gambling made food cheaper.

Of course non-gamblers—such as myself—were the real winners. We could eat well for very little, without giving back the gains at the slot machine. We enjoyed free parking and cheap hotel rooms for similar reasons.

Alas, this earlier system did not prove stable, and the cross-subsidy is now largely gone. Too many people, including town locals, ate the food, or stayed in the rooms, without gambling. Max Rubin wrote an entire book called *Comp City: A Guide to Free Casino Vacations*. He estimated that casinos were giving away half a billion dollars in value each year, and promised his readers $1 in benefits ("comps") for every 10 to 30 cents in gambling losses. Gamble just a bit, and promise to gamble more, and the casinos would treat you like a king.

Once people started to take advantage of the system, the casinos had to tighten up and limit the perks to proven gamblers. Casinos also built bigger hotels, such as the gargantuan Luxor, and used those rooms as a profit center. It no longer made sense to give away rooms to earn more from gambling. Shows, especially shows inside the big hotels, also proved to be moneymakers. As Las Vegas tried harder to lure families, gambling was no longer the major source of profits. Rather than using cheap rooms and cheap shows to lure gamblers, today's casinos use gambling to lure people to the rooms and the shows, the new profit centers.

Las Vegas gambling still subsidizes quality food, but only for the real gamblers. Casinos can identify top gamblers and they offer them—and only them—free meals at the top restaurants in their hotel/shopping complexes (and other perks). Everyone else must pay. The city now supports an outstanding selection of fine restaurants, including Chinois, Aureole, Emeril's, Le Cirque, Spago, Commander's Palace, and L'Atelier de Joël Robuchon, to name just a few. The best-known Las Vegas malls also have first-rate sushi, good Mexican food, and many other delicacies.

The resulting prices are often equal to or even higher than those for comparable food in New York City. This might seem surprising, given that Manhattan rents far exceed those in Vegas, but these high prices follow from the new relationship between food and gambling, or as the economist would say, from the new cross-subsidies. The casino compensates the restaurant every time a big gambler eats there for free. This payment boosts the demand for fine food. It is harder for everyone else to get a table, and thus prices rise. Furthermore, a "comped" gambler is more impressed by a free $150 meal than by a free $70 meal. The shopping malls, attached to casinos, will bid for restaurants with exorbitant and outlandish prices, if only to make their "gifts" to the top gamblers seem more generous.

It is no surprise that Las Vegas is now, after New York, America's location for fine dining and also America's location for expensive dining. But for all the wonders of Vegas food, the better buys are now in Singapore or Mexico.

· · ·

OKAY, THOSE ARE some tips for eating out, but what more can be said about cooking at home? I mentioned in an earlier chapter that I am the family cook. As the family cook, I take a real interest in cooking the right way, and the healthy way.

The first economic principle—and yes, it is an economic principle—is that you should eat healthy food at home. No, I don't mean this as another lecture against fat or on behalf of culinary puritanism. You're going to eat a certain amount of bad food no matter what, and I don't see it as my place in life to change that, even if I could. I eat unhealthy food too. I have a different point. Whatever amount of unhealthy eating you are going to do, *do it outside the home*. Restaurants are better at making food unhealthy. They know just how to add the right amounts of salt, fat, and sugar to the food. They have experience cooking for thousands, millions, or in the case of McDonald's, billions of customers. There is no good economic reason why you should master these same techniques.

Think of it as a way to master temptation and strengthen your inner self. Maybe you find it hard to resist unhealthy food when it is put before you, or when you see it on the menu at a restaurant. But you should find it eminently doable to resist learning how to make the stuff yourself. Really good French fries, after all, aren't easy and require some amount of training and practice. There is no need to put in that effort.

The second economic principle is not to take recipes too seriously. Treat them like art museums or "great" classic novels. Use them, abuse them, mock them, cackle at them, and scorn them. They're not necessarily put there to make you better off. To understand why this is true, let's walk through this point in a little more detail.

Usually our recipes come from cookbooks, from food magazines or newspapers, from the Internet, or perhaps from our friends. But if we are to enjoy life—and not just food—to the fullest, we should not take every recipe for granted. The person who wrote the recipe may not share our goals in every way. Recipe writers are not always altruists; many of them have their own agendas.

I can think of at least two motivations for recipes. First, some food recipes are designed to make us as happy as possible, taking into account the prices of the ingredients and the time and hassle involved in cooking. Think Rachael Ray and the thirty-minute meal. Second, some food recipes are designed to taste as good as possible, while ignoring our cost, time, and trouble. Hail the slow and careful braising of lamb, with foie gras and truffles to the side. And we had better whisk that butter sauce at just the right moment, or else. Do you own the right kind of blowtorch to make a good crème brûlée?

Cookbooks by famous chefs are more likely to fall into the second category. They seek to impress rather than to respect our limits. It may not look that way, but they have just a wee bit in common with James Joyce's *Finnegans Wake*.

Think about why this might be. The chef makes money not just from the cookbook but also from TV appearances, endorsements, and other products and activities. Their main goal is not to spare us time and trouble but rather to do the utmost to look like impressive chefs. That means their recipes will be too demanding. In other words, amateur cooks might resent having spent so much on the saffron, but if it tasted good they will praise the chef and his cookbook. Few people will visit the restaurant of a man who shows us how to find cheaper russet potatoes, no matter how valuable that information may be.

Knowing this, how should we adjust our personal cooking at home? Usually we should be just a little skeptical of fancy recipes. We could cut back on the most expensive ingredients, cut back on all ingredients, or perhaps add more spices and buy a lower quality of meat than suggested. At the very least we should cut back on our labor input and take shortcuts. This is in fact what most home cooks do, relative to the recipes they use. You don't really peel all those boiled almonds, do you? Don't feel guilty, just ponder the economic maximization problem, smile, and gulp down the final product.

If the recipe is old enough, it won't offer the right bundle of ingredients. Either new and better ingredients are available, or ingredients have changed with regard to their relative prices. Truffles weren't always as expensive as today. At the very least, wages have gone up over the last 200 years, and that means our time is more valuable. So if an old recipe calls for lots of time hunched over the stove, we should be especially skeptical.

If the recipe is from a supermarket, cut back on the expensive, high-margin items. Use more canned goods and less expensive cheese, relative to what is suggested.

The bottom line is this: just as enjoying a restaurant, or for that matter an art museum, does not come automatically, neither does enjoying a recipe. Whoever wrote the recipe has an agenda of her own. If you are to discover your Inner Economist in your own kitchen, start by figuring out the incentives of the author. Like many other things in this world, the recipe wasn't necessarily put there to make you happy. Grasping that fact and turning it to your advantage is a key step on the path to greater culinary delights.

8

Avoiding the Seven Deadly Sins (or Not)

ALL THE OTHER chapters in this book were about getting what you want. And the secret of that is to mobilize the Inner Economist. But we must fill in one further gap. Knowledge is only part of the problem—there is also willpower. Not everything we want is good for us. And I'm not just talking about French fries at McDonald's. I'm talking about sin. Thou shalt not . . .

This chapter doesn't have a major or startling recipe for self-improvement. It is instead a cautionary tale of how the learned still can go astray. It is a warning not to get too smug. It is designed to puncture hubris and bring us back to earth.

As an economist I appreciate the universality of markets and their close connection to almost every facet of human existence. The logic of markets has been with humankind since the dawn of recorded history and probably much further back. In a laboratory setting, even monkeys will engage in reciprocal cooperative behavior, if such conduct brings more food. Monkeys are also willing to trade Jell-O for grapes amongst each other. One Yale researcher is convinced that one of his monkeys traded sex (to another monkey) for a money token, which was then converted into a grape. Some monkeys are willing to give up food, just so they can gaze upon photos of other, high-status monkeys. This suggests that trading (and status-seeking) has deep roots in human nature.

Yes, markets are everywhere, but we also need to look twice at many of them—or rather, some are best avoided. Irresponsible behavior in markets is a growing problem. The proliferation and broader span of markets encourages many kinds of sin, and indeed sin seems to be more popular than ever before.

At any moment about 16 million items (on average) are for sale on eBay in the United States. These include markets in human needs, whims, fancies, dreams, and perversions. The modern world brings a baroque multiplication of the possible, spread through commercial space and designed to grab our attention. For just about every imaginable human desire or emotion—including the desire to sin—there are markets to be found. Of course sin is not always a sign of a bad life. If there is more sin in the world, it is in part because we have more opportunities, more wealth, and also more chances to (sometimes) make the right decisions.

For thousands of years human beings lived an essentially Malthusian existence, hovering at the verge of subsistence. Living standards would rise and fall, but Europeans in the early eighteenth century were not much better off than Europeans under the Roman Empire, if at all. And that picture was a grim one. If there was less sin, which I concede is debatable, it was because there was less of just about everything.

During the eighteenth and early nineteenth centuries, 50 to 75 percent of the typical European family budget was spent on food. Economist Robert Fogel reports that:

... the energy value of the typical diet in France at the start of the eighteenth century was as low as that of Rwanda in 1965, the most malnourished nation for that year in the tables of the World Bank.... As late as 1850, the English availability of calories hardly matched the current Indian level. One implication of these low-level diets needs to be stressed: Even prime-age males had only a meager amount of energy available for work ... the average efficiency of the human engine in Britain increased by about 53 percent between 1790 and 1980.

More calories, of course, mean more energy and, in addition, more sin. Lifetime sin also went up when human life expectancy passed forty years of age.

We should not become pessimistic about the fate of humanity simply because we see lots of sin in the modern world. We need to recognize that human beings are fallible, but of course at the same time we should not err in the opposite direction and forgive all behavior. If we are to cut back on harmful self-deception, we need to recognize that not everything we want is good for us. And it isn't easy.

This is not much of a "how-to" chapter. This is an "oh, please, let's not" chapter.

• • •

INSTEAD OF COURTING a real woman, some men prefer "imaginary girlfriends." Men may seek to please their mothers or impress work associates. How about making an ex—who is now living with another guy—a bit jealous?

Once a week these imaginary girlfriends—played by real women—will send you cards, e-mail, letters, or whatever else is needed to establish proof of a long-distance relationship. The idea started when a twenty-two-year-old named Judy, from Wichita Falls, Texas, posted her "imaginary" services on eBay; since then the idea has spread.

At Imaginarygirlfriends.com, after the period of hire has ended, the customer is responsible for splitting up with the imaginary girlfriend. The girlfriend will write a letter expressing her sorrow and begging to be taken back. At this point the customer is asked to ante up another payment, perhaps in search of a new imaginary girlfriend, if he has become sick of the old one.

The suppliers warn: "Anyone who has difficulty distinguishing reality from fantasy should NOT use this service."

The very beautiful Erica, from Vancouver, offers:

> Services: Letters, e-mail, custom photos with letters, custom digital photos with e-mail, video chats via Yahoo webcam if possible.
>
> Price $45 per two month period.

She is a big fan of classic rock, golf, and pro wrestling.

Some Japanese women are content with less than a full man. Such women can buy a "Boyfriend's Arm Pillow" to embrace their necks while they sleep at night. Japanese men can buy artificial women's laps, presumably to rest their heads in. The manufacturer advertises the ability of these laps to fulfill "primal needs."

Markets without values—or markets based on bad values—can misfire, with ugly results. Looking into the dark side, it is not hard to find markets—usually extensive and well-organized ones—for the ready-made categories of the Seven Deadly Sins. Dante's *Divine Comedy* (part II, "Purgatorio") is the best-known source for these sins, but the list dates at least as far back as Pope Gregory in the sixth century A.D., which explains their Latin names. Drawing upon this classical tradition, consider the following types of sinful (according to some) behavior and their associated markets:

I. Superbia (hubris/pride)

How did Andrew Skilling of Enron end up going to jail? He thought he could break the law with impunity and hide behind the success of his company. Few people expected that a company as large as Enron could unravel as quickly as it did. But formal instruction is offered to help executive criminals cope with the damage their hubris has wrought.

Top executives can take a class for $10,000 or more to learn how to cope with life in prison. The class teaches the following:

1. Meditation and physical-exercise routines.
2. Getting used to the fact that nothing changes and everything is outside your control.
3. Discarding addictions and vices.
4. Bringing a cheap watch.
5. Not making eye contact
6. "If you are going to hurt somebody, drag them into your cell, because then you have an excuse that they invaded your privacy."

The entrepreneurs claim they have had twelve clients a year for the last two years.

Remember the chapter on self-deception? Self-confidence can be a good motivator, but when accompanied by excess leverage, off-the-books partnerships, and phony accounting, watch out.

II. Avaritia (luxury/greed)

Aren't all markets based on greed to some extent? Maybe, but some markets are more brutal than others.

Kidnappers in the Philippines demand the names of two other

likely victims and an estimate of their net worth, before releasing children kidnapped from wealthy families. Kidnapping has been estimated to be a $200 million (tax-free) business in Colombia. Until the recent rise in safety, $1 million worth of Colombian kidnapping insurance cost $20,000 to $25,000 a year. Many people and companies buy much larger policies, for fear that the local kidnappers consider a ransom of less than a million to be a joke.

It is estimated that the fatality rate on security-consultant-handled kidnappings is about 2 percent. A victim is most likely to die if he or she cannot buy a release but must instead hope for a rescue. A victim is most likely to win a safe release when kidnapping is done in conjunction with the police. This minimizes the chance of misunderstandings and makes sure that everyone is on the same page. A victim's time in captivity is likely longest when the kidnappers are Marxist revolutionaries.

In Mexico the kidnappers and the insurance companies have a close working relationship. The kidnappers and the company will speak and a mutual transfer will be arranged. Since the parties have repeat business and "trust" each other, no one need send a chopped-off ear to establish the fact of the kidnapping. Not surprisingly, most kidnappers prefer to grab someone with insurance. That is their incentive, since the transaction runs more smoothly and everyone behaves professionally, or at least predictably. (There are, by the way, "rogue" kidnappers who behave nastily and spoil the market for everybody.) In essence the insurance company helps the kidnappers make credible commitments. The company certifies which kidnappers will in fact return a live body for the money, thereby making a transaction possible. The company is a kind of Better Business Bureau for the kidnappers; they won't just pay off any untutored rogues. The company "regularizes" the kidnapping experience, but at the same time this makes many kidnappings more likely and thus brings more sin.

Sometimes the greedy spend all their time looking for money, at the expense of virtually all other pursuits. We all expect there to be a market in "diamonds." But who would expect to find a market in "dimonds"? Alert arbitrageurs search eBay for misspelled and thus misplaced items. So if the lister made a mistake in the item description there will be few opposing bidders. One searcher bought Hubbell electrical cords for a tenth of their usual cost by searching for "Hubell" and "Hubbel" electrical cords. That same individual bought Compaq computers by looking for "Compacts" instead.

One reporter's hour-long search turned up dozens of items, including "bycicles," "telefones," "mother of perl," "cuttlery," "bedroom suits," and "antiks."

One seller listed a chandelier, but was unsure how to spell it. She did a Web search, which confirmed some results for her spelling intuition of "chandaleer" (circa 2007, I find 2,850 listings for this spelling). The listing went up and some alert bidder received a bargain.

There is now a Web site, eBooboos.com, devoted solely to finding and publicizing spelling mistakes on eBay. This is a useful service, but it is also a Web site for the greedy.

III. Luxuria (extravagance, later lust)

In Mexico City there are hundreds of prostitutes in their sixties, seventies, and even eighties; eighty-five is the oldest age cited. One woman claims that: "an antique can be more valuable than something new." Usually the price is $5 or less. If there are markets in anything, there are markets in lust.

For a $34 minimum a Russian company will provide an alibi for the absence of an adulterer. Sometimes a person might wish to hide from his or her significant other. A service named SounderCover gives the user the ability to add background sounds to a phone call. The purpose is to give the impression that the user is somewhere else rather than, say, having an affair with his mistress. The service can mimic traffic, construction noises, the circus, or the drill of a dentist.

Celebrities, athletes, and others can buy consent forms for their casual sex partners. The form vouches that the other party agreed to the sex, thereby avoiding subsequent charges of rape or harassment. "This really is for someone you don't know," noted lawyer Evan Spencer, who drafted the "pre-sexual agreement" form for Protect Condoms, Inc. According to the president of the company, they rapidly sold more than 4,000 forms at $7.99 per form. Each package comes with two condoms. It sounds useful, but in reality it probably just makes people more likely to commit mistakes. It doesn't protect against stalkers, bruised feelings, or ruined marriages.

Lust and drunkenness often go together. We have all known people who make phone calls when they shouldn't, especially when they are drunk. A survey of 409 people by Virgin Mobile found that 95 percent had made drunk calls, mostly to ex-partners (30 percent), 19 percent to current partners, and 36 percent to others, including their bosses. Fifty-five percent of those people looked at their phones the next morning to see whom they had called—similarly, someone is waking up in the world this minute and checking to see who it is he or she is sleeping with.

To alleviate the drinking-and-dialing problem, a phone company in Australia started offering customers blocked "blacklist" numbers, which they select before going out to drink. In Japan they sell a mobile phone with a breathalyzer, to see if you are really fit to drive home, or for that matter to make a phone call. If a bus driver fails the test, his location is sent immediately to his boss by GPS.

IV. Invidia (envy)

Many market purchases—from a Mercedes to a $5,000 purse—are motivated by envy, usually of our immediate peers or neighbors. My professorial colleagues are upset by the raises given to people down the hall, but they don't much seem to mind the wealth of Bill Gates or the Sultan of Brunei.

Advertisements often try to persuade us that if we buy the product we will make our neighbors jealous. PartyBuddys, the creation of two New Jersey entrepreneurs, promises to "make normal people feel fabulous for the night." This does not involve an economics lecture, a sermon, or advice on how to best help the poor. Instead, the one-night package offers a special "party buddy" guide to bring clients past "crowds of jealous bystanders," limousine transportation, and special treatment at six fashionable Manhattan nightclubs, including free drinks. One night costs $350 a person and up; the maximum package goes for $1,200 per person. A personal bodyguard runs an extra $45 an hour.

The managers of the business estimate that at least 60 percent of their business comes from middle-aged professionals who are visiting New York but have never been to the city's nightclubs. For one night this exotic adventure allows these status-conscious customers to imagine themselves as one of "the cool people" they see on TV. New Yorkers, of course, consider this the epitome of uncool.

A report from India tells of a firm that rents out wedding guests, so that the wedding and the party do not look empty. The "guests" will wear either traditional Indian dress or Western clothes, depending on what the customer dictates. They are told to dance and make small talk, and show a knowledge of the marrying couple, without letting on that they are hired. The firm's owner, a Mr. Syed, told one newspaper: "The breaking up of joint families and lack of affection among relatives also creates a demand for paid guests." The Best Guests Centre, at Jodhpur in Rajasthan, is looking to expand.

To each his own; I would pay some people to stay away from my wedding.

V. Gula (gluttony)

As you will have noticed, I like eating. But there is a restaurant in China that specializes in serving different kinds of animal penises, braised, fried, and steamed. I am eager to visit, but not eager to eat there.

The World Grilled Cheese Eating Championship offers a $3,500 prize to the contestant who can down the greatest number of grilled-cheese sandwiches in ten minutes. The 103-pound Korean-American Sonya ("The Black Widow") Thomas won with twenty-three. Jason Fagone's 302-page study of eating competitions, *Horsemen of the Esophagus*, used the words "violent" and "assault" to describe the contestants' methods of consumption. He notes that Sonya has no "recognizable style" because "she knows that style bleeds speed." Sonya, considered by many to be the world's premier competitive speed eater, exercises up to two hours a day on a treadmill. She eats only one (very large) meal a day, which takes her several hours. She worked at Burger King and would like to own a fast-food restaurant some day.

To me this just sounds stupid, but how many people approve of my quest to find the very best Mexican street food, regardless of the risk of an upset stomach or worse?

VI. Ira (wrath)

Markets in murder, arms sales, and terrorist killings can be found on the news virtually every day. Halting or slowing down wrath is one of the hardest problems we face in the world. Enough said.

VII. Acedia (sloth)

Is sloth always a sin? Probably not. Some amount of leisure is good for us, and is fun as well. But the quiet seventh deadly sin can be taken to an extreme.

Today a wealthy person can hire an aide to do virtually *anything*. Many of these tasks are reasonable—does not capitalism require division of labor?—but David Beckham and his wife hired a £1,000-a-day butler to open their Christmas presents. Prince Charles had a full-time valet at the age of two and he still has his butler apply toothpaste to his toothbrush.

Some people purchase software to play online computer games for them. Why bother? If "you" have played the game, you can wear certain badges attesting to that fact, which leads to prestige in some online communities.

At some luxury hotels it is possible to have a massage therapist summoned right to the golf course. Some Ritz-Carltons offer their guests constant e-mail contact with their butlers, who carry around handheld wireless devices.

This may not sound all that bad. Maybe these services are making the person more productive. Maybe these services are signaling just how important the person is. But maybe they also signal a lack of good judgment.

· · ·

OF COURSE THE seven deadly sins are hardly an exclusive list. The modern world comes up with new and more enticing ways to sin, and then markets those opportunities. Taking a cue from a classical Greek and Roman moral code rather than a Christian one, we can find markets in overcoming cowardice. Want to feel rugged or tough? The company

BSR offers a two-day antiterrorist driving school, which includes surveillance and 180-degree spins. Gift certificates are available.

A three-day antiterrorist camp in Arizona teaches espionage and combat pistol techniques for only $3,800. They offer a special course on Russian martial arts, promising that for the course, "if you do spend time in a hotel, it won't be a five-star." You learn the "Systema" method of self-defense, dating (supposedly) from the Russian Cossacks, enabling you to strike from virtually any position. Their driving adventures include lessons in Southern truck-racing.

Of course not everyone is a rogue or a tough guy. Many of us live in fear, and markets cater to that personality type as well.

Sometimes we are too cowardly to face those we have loved and maybe even still love. At www.breakupservice.com, founded in 2002, the writers pen a Dear John or Dear Jane letter designed to end the relationship. But if a letter is too impersonal, better to hire the service for a fifteen-minute breakup phone call, called a "counseling call" by the service. Many call recipients first react by thinking it is a joke. But in the words of the service founder, once they get over this impression they find it is "a learning experience." He also remarks: "They have an inkling there's a problem. Now they have some real closure with real answers. We try to help them look at it as a new beginning."

The company once received the following testimonial:

> I met what I thought was a sweet girl. We dated a couple of times then I realized she was completely psycho. She would not take any of the hints I gave as I didn't want her around but one phone call with a follow-up letter from breakupservice.com did the trick. I never heard from her again. Thanks! Charlie M.

Another of these companies also performs furniture and pet retrieval, for fees ranging up to $400.

The now-defunct LadyLoveWriter.com—and its male-oriented counterpart LoveWriter.com—offered to compose "The Gentle Break-up Letter" for a client. A direct mail copywriter speaks to the client on the phone and e-mails an appropriate breakup letter to the customer, who then sends it in his or her own handwriting, or perhaps just uses "cut and paste."

Customers who commissioned such letters had to supply the answers to eight informational questions about what kind of message is desired. It also had to be specified whether the style should be "Light and Casual," "Straightforward but from the Heart," or "Super-Romantic." Erica Klein, the founder of the service, noted, "We're good at caring and compassion."

Taphephobia (or "taphophobia," depending which spelling convention you follow) is the fear of being buried alive. A Chilean cemetery will build an alarm into a coffin for only $462. In 1995 entrepreneurs marketed a $5,000 Italian casket with an emergency signal beeper and a two-way microphone/speaker to the outside world. The accompanying survival kit includes a torch, an oxygen tank, and a heart stimulator; don't ask who will administer the latter.

Markets also cater to many extreme forms of vanity, another classical sin. For instance, we can buy testicular implants for our pets. Apparently some pet owners feel their dogs have lost that manly feeling or that dangerous look. To date at least 50,000 people have purchased this product.

To take it one step further:

> For her 17th wedding anniversary Jeanette Yarborough wanted to do something special for her husband. In addition to planning a hotel getaway for the weekend, Ms. Yarborough paid a surgeon $5,000 to reattach her hymen, making her appear to be a virgin again.
>
> "It's the ultimate gift for the man who has everything," says Ms. Yarborough.

This is reported to be one of the plastic-surgery industry's fastest-growing segments, and yes, that is in the United States. Our culture is not very good at constraining or regulating vanity.

• • •

MARKETS NEVER COVER or offer all options, if only because of economic and legal constraints. Economists refer to "transaction costs" and "fixed costs." Most of these constraints are weakening over time, and thus we witness an intensifying proliferation of markets, including those cited above. That places a greater burden on our faculties of self-control.

Transaction costs reflect the difficulty of bringing together buyers and sellers and getting them to agree on terms. For instance, I continue to look for an extra copy of the CD *The Kampala Sound*, a collection of top Ugandan tunes from the 1960s. The Web fails me, and even Original Music, the issuer, claims to have no back copies. But finding a seller may just be a matter of time. The Internet is causing transaction costs to fall to ever-lower levels. FedEx, fax machines, credit bureaus, eBay buyer ratings, and cheaper air travel all make it easier to cut deals and move the goods.

Sometimes the parties to an exchange come together quite easily and through established channels. For $430 a square foot, a person can buy the air rights for an unfettered view of Central Park. That means no one can build to block the current view. This transaction operates through the standard real estate brokers of Manhattan.

In contrast, men who wish to buy paintings made by women's breasts (N.B.: not paintings *of* women's breasts, these are paintings *by* the breasts) must transact outside the mainstream. The idea, which started on the Internet, allows a small number of buyers to get in touch with the willing but regionally dispersed artistic suppliers. This is now possible because transaction costs have fallen.

Some of today's newest and most innovative markets exist in online computer games. In these "synthetic worlds" it is possible to buy, sell, lend, own property, or for that matter steal. Rewards depend upon performance, and the game prizes are convertible into real-world cash. It has been estimated that all the synthetic economies put together, with about 10 million players, are in value terms about equal to the size of the economies of Bosnia and Herzegovina. Ten years ago, these games did not exist.

The "fixed costs" idea—another limit on markets—is a little more difficult to define than transaction costs, but we all understand it intuitively through our Inner Economist. Fixed costs are the reason why we don't see many walk-in, quirky bohemian bookshops in rural Nebraska. There just aren't enough buyers to cover the basic expenses of operation. But like transaction costs, fixed costs have been falling rapidly, and for many of the same reasons.

Even though more markets are possible than ever before, our legislators have decided that there should not be markets in everything. Laws curtail voluntary exchange in ecstasy, sexual intercourse, kidneys for transplant, betting on numbers, and many supposed cures for cancer. It is very difficult to find the best unpasteurized French cheeses in the United States; the FDA has decided they are not good for us.

Of course, many of these markets proceed with or without legal support. Prostitutes advertise freely in the Yellow Pages; the police usually tolerate the practice as long as the neighbors do not complain. (If the customers can find these prostitutes, surely the police can, too.) If you want to move to the front of the queue for a kidney, donate a large sum of money to the hospital.

During America's experiment with Prohibition, it was common to see the following label on grape juice:

Caution: May Ferment into Alcohol.

The harvesting of grapes rose dramatically.

Many markets are designed to help people avoid or circumvent lawful regulations. One British entrepreneur sells squirt bottles of spray-on mud for license plates. It is ostensibly so the buyer's vehicle can "look rugged," but more realistically it is used so police cameras cannot record the license plates of speeding vehicles. The mud is from Shropshire, and it contains secret ingredients so that it sticks to the license plate longer.

Of course these costs are not the only or even the primary obstacles to exchange; sometimes human beings are outraged by the idea of trading everything in markets as I've touched on in earlier chapters.

Sometimes we feel squeamish, even morally outraged, about buying and selling certain rights and privileges. Felix Oberholzer-Gee, a professor at Harvard Business School, conducted some field experiments about whether a market might develop for places in line.

Some economists might think that buying a place in line is a natural thing to do. Some people mind waiting in line more than others. Some of us are simply less patient by temperament. Other times we wish to avoid lines to avoid missing a flight or an important appointment. If the flight leaves in fifteen minutes and the airport security line is long, our temptation is to run to the front of the line, screaming for mercy and perhaps waving a few dollar bills. Yet it turns out to be remarkably hard to buy a better place in line.

Oberholzer-Gee and a team of experimenters set out with some money in their pockets. They went to long lines and offered cash payments of up to $10 if they could cut in line, jumping ahead of some of the others.

The higher the payment offered, the more likely that the researcher was allowed to cut into the line. But most people would not take the money. They took a high offer as a signal of desperation and thus felt sorry for the interloper and let him cut in for nothing. (Students and women were more likely to take the cash; men were more likely to "act magnanimously.") So the original order of the queue was not seen as sacrosanct, but most people felt it was not right to receive cash for an early spot in line. They were willing to help someone in need, but did not wish to profit from that assistance.

That said, people in the queue felt only limited generosity. When a *second* experimenter—this time the professor himself rather than his assistant—tried to buy his way into the line, those in the queue grew upset. Even people who let one outsider buy into the line stopped at the second offer. Many went further and challenged the desire of the researcher to push himself forward. In fact the professor felt obliged to retreat from the situation, to avoid being slugged, pushed, or otherwise hurt. When people felt their generosity was being taken advantage of, they did not allow the outsiders to exploit the situation, with or without a cash payment.

A study led by Nobel Laureate Daniel Kahneman—based on intensive time diaries—looked at which activities make us happiest. It turns out that sex and time spent with friends (not spouses, unless perhaps we are having sex) are our favorite and most enjoyable ways of spending time. Children do not rank highly in terms of making us happy in the moment, although arguably they bring long-term satisfaction with life.

A second study, by economists David Blanchflower and Andrew Oswald, supports the view of a connection between sex and happiness. A random sample of 16,000 adult Americans finds "that sexual activity enters strongly positively in happiness equations."

(By the way, this paper offers other fascinating results. Greater income buys neither more sex nor more sexual partners. The typical American has intercourse two or three times a month. Married people have more sex on average. Sex is more closely correlated with happiness if the person is highly educated. The happiest people had but a single sexual partner last year. Education lowers the number of sexual partners a woman will have. Homosexuality has no statistically significant effect on happiness.)

If sex is so much more fun than the alternatives, why don't we have more of it? Why do we watch as much TV as we do, or putter around in the basement, instead of having more sex?

The economist will be satisfied only with gains-from-trade-defying reasons. Maybe the potential partner is not interested right now but, hey, is that not what trade is for? Nonetheless I can think of a few possible explanations—some weaker, some stronger—for why people do not have more sex:

1. The long-term lifestyle costs of being "more open to trading sex" involve a loss of integrity and control.
2. We have enough sex, and more sex would be much less fun (economics lingo: the average utility of sex is high, but the marginal utilities are diminishing rapidly). Okay, this may be true on a given night, but the U.S. average is only two or three nights a month.
3. Freud was right and we are repressed. The will is not unitary and the part of the self in control does not care much about happiness. Many theories of evolutionary psychology make a similar prediction.
4. Sex stops being enjoyable when we do it "to close a gap between marginal utilities." It requires spontaneity or some other quality inconsistent with the traditional economic model of the consumer. Imagine telling a girlfriend that you have a burning desire to "equate your marginal rates of substitution," as a mathematically oriented economist might describe it.
5. Sex isn't as much fun as the studies indicate. Perhaps people lie about the quality of their sex or remember only the better experiences.
6. People want their sex to consist of peaks, rather than seeking to

maximize lifetime pleasure. Thomas Schelling once told me he does not always listen to Bach, even when he feels like doing so. He wants to keep it as a special experience.

7. The market-clearing price for more sex is positive. Overall men want sex more than women do, plus many women are more selective in their choice of partner. Many men are bidding, implicitly or explicitly, for a smaller number of women. Yet people feel shame about paying or receiving money in too explicit a fashion (see also #4). We therefore spend our time competing for social status, rather than just trading for more sex. We keep this tendency even after we have settled with a partner.

8. During and after marital fights, we often "stick to our guns." Some of our stubbornness is for purposes of deterrence and precedent-setting. If we give in too easily, we will find it harder to win a good bargain the next time around. The result is mutual stubbornness, excess self-righteousness, and less sex than might otherwise be the case.

No matter which explanations we favor, we can see that exchanging sex is, upon examination, not so simple. We love (some kinds of) sex, yet we cannot just go out and trade for more.

The lessons are evident. Transaction costs, fixed costs, and the law are less important constraints on our behavior than in times past. Yet we shouldn't make every possible trade that comes before us. Even when sex is at stake. Sometimes our Inner Economist simply ought to say no.

I am a strong believer in an ethic of individual responsibility, so I do not think we can or that we should look primarily to the law to prevent our moral mistakes. In many areas of life, people need to be free to fail if their lives are to have meaning, or if virtue is to be possible. Often paternalistic laws cannot be adequately enforced, or those laws create harmful and counterproductive black markets.

No matter what options markets offer, social regulation has to start at the level of the rationally prudent self.

. . .

I'VE HEARD OF plenty of tricks to encourage self-control. Many of these tricks use markets, typically markets in preventive devices of some kind.

One device, called the DDS System, resembles a small retainer that you put into your mouth before mealtime. It fills much of the upper cavity of the mouth and forces the wearer to eat more slowly and take smaller bites. The product is marketed by Scientific Intake of Atlanta and is supposed to be fitted with dental supervision. The makers claim the effect on speech is "minor"; the effect on your pocketbook is $400 to $500. The device was originally modeled after an affliction called torus palatinus, which is a bulge of bone growing from the center of the palate. A woman with such a bone claims it hindered her eating and thus kept her thin for life. Thus was born a new patent and then a new product. The company admits that product use can be circumvented by drinking milk shakes and other high-calorie beverages.

Other gimmicks come from digital culture. For instance, pornography addicts can download free "accountability software" known as X3. Once installed, X3 sends an e-mail every fourteen days to a chosen recipient or recipients. That e-mail lists every Web site that the person has visited on the computer.

There is lots of ingenuity in the marketplace, but most of these tricks do not work in the long run or are counterproductive. We rely on the gimmick instead of developing a healthier way of life and a better approach to making decisions. The technology or the trick distracts us from strengthening our will. Hiding the Lindt dark chocolate from myself doesn't work, and in fact it often just makes me want the candy all the more.

Here are three pieces of advice on overcoming self-control problems:

First, cultivate a healthy self-image and a set of narratives about who you are and why it is important to contribute to society, rather than yielding to every temptation. The earlier chapter about the dangerous and necessary art of deceiving yourself considers self-narratives in more detail, as does the next chapter about saving the world. In a nutshell, develop a constructive alternative for helping the world and talk yourself into believing it matters. Who knows, maybe it really does matter.

Second, train yourself to use the better and more wholesome markets, of which there are plenty. Forget about the imaginary girlfriend, the Russian alibi for adultery, and the Mexican prostitutes. Just go out and look for some sweet, old-fashioned romance.

Yes, virtue is its own reward, but virtue also should be fun. Go out and use markets to make virtue fun. Buy a nice home for you and your family.

The third lesson is the simplest and most fundamental of them all. Don't say yes to everything. Don't use every market that looks fun or exciting. Make a judgment for yourself about what really matters to you. Act on it. Exercise self-control.

And if you make the wrong decisions, well, there is a new market that you might want to turn to. The truly regretful in the Chinese city of Nanjing can visit a "crying bar." There's a sofa, some tables, and a great deal of tissue paper. For about $6 an hour, customers can sit and cry. The owner, one Luo Jun, claimed he hit upon the idea from customers of a previous bar. They wanted to cry, but they had no venue for this desire. The crying bar solves their problem by making the show of maudlin emotion socially respectable and indeed socially expected.

I hope I don't see you there.

9

How to Save the World—
More Christmas Presents Won't Work

IT HAS LONG been thought that to save the world you have to devote your life to a new approach to something. You may be searching for a cure for cancer or a way to produce clean and cheap energy. Most of us feel that even after work is over, we would like to be charitable and do something altruistic. We want to give.

It is often believed, however, that economists are narrow and selfish. Indeed we cannot dismiss the idea that the study of economics corrupts people. Many key economic concepts, such as gross domestic product, are measured in terms of dollars and cents. Most economics is based around the notions that consumers "maximize utility" and that firms "maximize profit." What could sound less charitable than that?

One economist—Joel Waldfogel—wrote a paper measuring and apparently criticizing the "deadweight loss" resulting from Christmas gifts. Did we really want those new kitchen bowls? According to his calculations, the American economy loses about $4 billion in value per year by giving gifts at Christmas. Those who are not professors of economics might get the impression that these dismal scientists are opposed to the very idea of festive holidays.

Data from the laboratory support the caricature of economists as selfish. Cornell University researcher Robert Frank asked economics students to play a variety of games for monetary prizes. The rewards the student received depended on how much he or she was willing to play noncooperative strategies at the expense of competitors. In these games, the individuals who had studied economics behaved more selfishly and less cooperatively than the control group. Furthermore a given student, after studying economics, played more selfishly than before. Maybe some of the students thought they were supposed to play this way, to look good to the instructor.

Some of the blame rests with the economists. Our science—or should I say our art?—is so often used for selfish purposes. D.H. Robertson asked in 1954 "What Does the Economist Economize?" and he concluded that the final answer was love. But few economists have heeded this perspective. It is easier to study selfish behavior because it is easier to recognize, easier to measure, and also easier to bill for consulting fees.

Charity is an understudied part of developed economies. In 2005 Americans contributed more than $260 billion to philanthropic and charitable organizations. That is more than two percent of the economy. This figure does not include the $28.4 billion of remittances sent to other countries from the United States. Nor does it include volunteering or our casual charity on the street, neither of which makes its way onto our tax returns.

In per capita terms, Norway and Denmark give the most government-to-government foreign aid. Norwegians are the most likely to offer their time—a stunning 52 percent of the adult population volunteers in some manner; the United Kingdom is next in line with 30 percent. (If you are wondering, of the cited countries Mexico comes in last with a volunteering rate of 0.1 percent.)

Suppose we wish to go out and do the world some good. How might our Inner Economist help us be better altruists? I will consider this problem one angle at a time, but some common themes will recur. To get good results we must ask what is truly scarce. We must ask how people—both donors and recipients—will respond to incentives. We must confront our true motivations and distinguish between doing the world good versus feeling better about ourselves.

• • •

ASSUME THAT WE have some money to give away, but we do not have time to manage any charitable projects. We just want to give the money away and be done with it. To whom should the money go?

I faced this dilemma when I first visited India in 2004. I have traveled to about seventy foreign countries, including five trips to Haiti, a trip around West Africa, and about a dozen trips to rural Mexico. So I was familiar with privation.

Yet nothing had prepared me for India. Here was extreme poverty on a scale of the many millions. And unlike in most of Africa, the crowding was extreme. The air was a mix of smells from burning charcoal, rotting garbage, human urine, and excrement. For all the (justified) talk about India on the rise, most of the country still lives with medieval technology but modern levels of crowding. Non-mechanized agriculture remains the dominant economic sector. Did I mention that to start a small business in India, it takes an average of eighty-nine days to get the relevant permits and legal permissions? The cost of this trouble is about half of yearly per capita income in India.

At first I could not understand why so many of the streets, even the streets with no nearby stores or attractions, were so full of people. I soon realized those people were *living* on the streets. If I couldn't see their possessions, it was probably because they didn't have any.

Calcutta (now Kolkata, but I will use the former and better-known name) was the most extreme example of poverty and crowding I encountered. The recent Indian boom came to Calcutta later than in other parts of India. The surrounding state of Bengal has had socialist and communist governments for a long time, and not to its advantage. Calcutta also appears to have a better developed "culture of begging," perhaps because it was the original capital of the British Empire in India. The very poor have had begging "targets" for a longer period of time than in, say, Bombay (Mumbai). Walking down the main street in front of my hotel meant being importuned a dozen times within the span of a minute.

Children as young as six or seven will ask for money in the few words of English they have learned. Cripples lay on the sidewalk, waving their stumps for sympathy. They will carry a sign—carefully scrawled—even if they are in no position to proposition more aggressively. Mothers approach with small babies wrapped to their chests. Every time my cab stopped, people like these approached the windows.

But should we give beggars money? It seems heartless not to give anything. After all, we have so much and they have so little. We can see that they are hungry. For less than a dollar they can eat for a few days; lentils and rice are cheap. We wouldn't even notice if that dollar were gone. It is not a dollar we will spend on an ice cream cone or a song on iTunes. It is a rounding error for most of us. If you don't think so, try telling me how many dollars you have in your pocket or around the house. How about in your checking account?

When it comes to beggars, many religious prophets have recommended charity. On the other hand, I often have heard from tourist guides (and from my mother, for that matter) that we should not give money to beggars, because "it only encourages them to beg." There is a grain of truth to this argument, but it doesn't really nail the answer. So what if we encourage them to beg? Isn't begging—and receiving something—better than dying of starvation? Isn't the whole point to encourage starving people to get some money?

The economist approaches the problem by asking a pointed question: how hard will beggars work to get your money? In Calcutta the answer was simple. They worked pretty hard, relative to what they received. They would stake out favorable space on the street corner, defend that space against other beggars, try to learn some English, chase stopped cabs, draw up begging signs, and so on. If nothing else, becoming a beggar keeps many people from living in a more salubrious part of town, or near a cheaper source of food.

The problem with giving to beggars is that we encourage them to chase after the money. Say a street corner in Calcutta yields about $100 a year in begging income. How hard will a beggar work to command that street corner? It is difficult to answer this question with precision, but it is easy to see that a beggar might have to invest up to $100 to get and keep that corner, especially if other beggars want the same space. So if tourists are giving $100 and the beggar is spending $100 to keep the post, the net gain to the beggar is zero.

It gets worse. It has long been rumored that many Indian beggars cut off their limbs or induce gangrene to generate sympathy and thus earn more money. Such claims are hard to verify, but recently a "sting" was set for several Indian doctors. Men dressed up as beggars visited doctors and asked to have their limbs amputated. Three surgeons were filmed agreeing to perform the necessary work. The price for taking off a lower leg was about 10,000 rupees, or $215. One doctor also asked the man whether he might like three fingers of his left hand chopped off. It is reputed that some doctors know how to stitch up blood vessels in a limb to induce it to blacken with gangrene.

Most beggars don't go so far. But even if a beggar invests $50 of effort to earn $100, the net gain is only $50. There is a better way to give away the money.

The truth is this: the more we give to beggars, the harder beggars will try. This leads to what economists call (awkwardly) "rent exhaustion," which limits the net value created by the donation.

We also should ask how many more people will flow into the begging trade if the earnings of beggars go up. In Calcutta at least, begging is a profession, much like shining shoes. More donations induce more Bengalis to take up begging. This brings the return to begging back down. Our donations might create a transitory gain for some beggars, but the next year our beggar friends will take in correspondingly less money.

Instead of targeting beggars we should give our money to the needy who are not trying very hard. Economists call these the "relatively inelastic factors"; the word "inelastic" means they are not spending their time chasing our dollars. (Intuitively, their behavior does not "stretch" much, thus the "inelastic" jargon.) This usually rules out beggars, who are looking for a buck and respond to incentives very quickly.

If you are going to give, pick the poor person who is expecting it least. Give to Bengalis who are sleeping, Bengalis who are cooking, and Bengalis who are otherwise occupied doing something from normal life. It is not hard to find very poor Bengalis engaged in all of these activities. It is quite easy to find a Bengali sleeping under a piece of cardboard. We will know we have picked the right person if the object of our generosity is totally surprised. The surprise means he or she was not eating up valuable time and energy angling for a donation.

Under this approach, we give to those who do not ask. This is harder for many of us. It requires us to be proactive. And when the beggars do ask, we end up saying no. We turn away when they stare at us in the taxicab. We feel bad. We don't feel so guilty when we turn down the kindly Bengali gentleman sleeping under the piece of cardboard. He never pushed his predicament in front of our face. But if we really want to help others—and *be* nice rather than just feeling like a nice guy—that is where our money should go.

If all tourists were to follow this advice, we might need to spread around our giving. For instance, if all tourists give to people who are cooking, the end result would be large and wasteful displays of Indian cooking out on the streets of Calcutta. If everyone tries to "surprise" recipients in the same manner, it won't be a surprise at all. What we need to do—in our role as benefactor—is to find a new and unusual way to get resources in the hands of poor Bengalis.

There are, of course, exceptions. Sometimes we *should* give money to those who ask for it. In some more formal charitable settings, competition for our dollars is desirable. New York City's Metropolitan Opera has a strong fund-raising network. This, in part, reflects the quality of the institution and its music. If they send a Christmas letter asking for funds, we should not recoil in horror. We might instead treat the letter and the fund-raising campaign as a signal of their broader competence in running the organization.

But we should not make a comparable inference about the beggar. The beggars who solicit us in Calcutta may be good at fighting for a spot on the street, but this competence does not mean much. If we want to give money to the competent, we should seek out a Bengali running a sweets shop. Beggars are playing the "needy game" and signaling their distress, not their abilities to turn our money into a small fortune.

In other cases a solicitation for funds might make us aware that a problem exists in the first place. I had not known of pyruvoyl-tetrahydropterin synthase deficiency until recently, though perhaps the doctors working on the problem deserve my support. How many Americans could describe the symptoms and results of lupus? A fund-raising campaign may inform us. But again this logic does not apply to the beggars in Calcutta. We all know about these beggars and their poverty even before we step foot in India.

Begging has been around for a very long time, and it is found in many parts of the world. That so many religions address it is evidence of how strong a role it plays in human nature. Given its import, how we respond to begging reflects the central distinction between "wanting to feel we are doing some good" and "doing some good." We should not let "feel good" self-deception keep us from actually making a difference. Yet at the same time we must keep our interest in the problem of poverty from slipping away, and yes that means we need to feel good about our giving. What is the best way to achieve that end?

• • •

THE ABOVE ADVICE is good for our trips, but those are special occasions. We experience some kind of begging almost every day. We cannot avoid being asked for money just by sitting in our living rooms. Charitable requests will find us, if only through the mail or a phone call. *Should* we give to the Metropolitan Opera?

In a typical week I receive in the mail about five solicitations for funds. Some call it "direct mail," and others call it "junk mail." No one knows exactly how many pieces of charitable mail are sent each year. Sixty-five billion pieces of direct mail are sent every year in the United States, but many of these are commercial rather than charity mailings. We do know that the nonprofit sector in the United States relies heavily on mass mailings. Data privacy issues make mailings less important in Europe by restricting the use of names and addresses (usually recipient consent is required before the mailing occurs). Nonetheless European charities are growing and they, like their counterparts in the United States, stage benefits, use social networking, and send people out on personal visits. They spend money trying to get money, and the same economic logic applies to their activities.

When should we give to such pleas? The first rule is to give to causes that we will become attached to. If our goal is truly to help people, bad charities are not the foremost problem. We—that's right, you and I—usually are enemy number one. Over time most people lose interest in charitable causes. Not for any good reason, but we simply stop caring. Images of catastrophe and stories of suffering fade. Charitable giving becomes an abstraction, set against the very real and pressing demands of our daily lives. If we really want to do the world some good, we need to stop ourselves from becoming indifferent in the future.

We are returning to the economist's question: what is the relevant scarcity? And how do we best address that scarcity? In this case, the relevant scarcity is people who really care. Our giving should become akin to an addiction. If we have started to give, and then we stop, it should hurt. It should make us feel bad, as if we had abandoned family members.

Of course, fund-raisers are happy to get us hooked on giving, and yes this does make the world a better place. Most (reputable) charities won't tell us we are rotten when we don't give, but they will tell us we are wonderful when we do give. They send donors Christmas cards, letters of praise, and special plaques. Get used to that feeling and enjoy it.

● ● ●

IF WE FIND a worthy cause and a worthy charity, we should stick with it. Loyalty to our causes makes charities more financially effective. Charities make most of their money off what is called a "house file." The house file consists of donors who have been giving loyally for years. A good house file is like gold. It brings in much more than it costs to maintain.

Let us return to the theme of what is truly scarce in this context. From the charity's point of view, it is very hard to find donors who are interested in giving at all. Let's say that a charity sends direct mail or otherwise solicits a rented list of names. Not surprisingly, the response rate on direct mail is very low. In fact, a 1 percent response rate is considered a success in many cases. Furthermore the mailing costs money. Names must be rented, letters must be drawn up and printed, and of course the postal service raises its prices all the time.

If a mailing brings in thirty cents for every dollar spent, that mailing probably went relatively well by the standards of the sector. A fifty-cent return per dollar spent is a smashing hit.

Why spend a dollar to get thirty or fifty cents? The answer is simple: the charity is investing in developing its house file. Some of those new donors will "stick," and in the future they will give much more. In economic terms, the "expected present value" of a new but loyal donor is high.

Of course not every charity finds new donors by direct mail. Networking among friends and acquaintances also generates new support. But the same logic will apply. No matter what the cause, it is very costly to find new donors. Once donors are on the books, they add a great deal of value.

The practical import is this: we benefit charities—if we can find good ones—by sticking in their house files and continuing to give. Otherwise charities are spending more money on us than we are worth.

We now have a new way to make the world a better place. Once we have found some good charities, we should tell them not to rent out our name and address to other mailers. Virtually all charities rent out or swap names and addresses to similar groups; what better way is there to find new donors than to look for people who are already giving to related causes?

"Remove the name" requests save charities thousands of dollars on their mailing costs. Consider some quick estimates. Let us say that you would otherwise receive one piece of charitable junk mail a week, a conservative estimate if you have been giving to charities. That single piece of mail costs a charity, on average, in the range of fifty cents to $2 per piece, depending on the quality of the mailing. It is well-known in the sector that donors are more likely to respond when the letter is on nice paper, long, and the envelope looks like a personalized invitation. Renting the names can cost another dollar, although this expense is minimized if lists are swapped with other charities.

That one piece of mail a week involves mailing costs of $25 to $100 over a year. If you are getting five pieces a week, the numbers go up to

$125 to $500 in mailing costs over the year. And neither of those figures includes the possible costs of name rental. So the single act of taking your name off mailing lists creates charitable value of at least $50—maybe more—over the course of a year. Over a lifetime this could add up to hundreds or maybe thousands of dollars.

Just limiting these mailings is one of the most cost-effective means of contributing to charity. It costs no more than the stamp and the time to write the letter, or perhaps a free e-mail. Given how mailings work, we need only get our names off those lists of the charities we support. Our initial charities do not, or at least should not, sell our actual names and addresses. Instead the names are rented to a third-party broker, which mails a solicitation on behalf of another cause but does not pass the names along to the charity renting the names. So we need not track down every charity that mails to us; we only have to catch the charities that have our addresses.

Of course this entire procedure assumes that we've already found the causes we love and support. Maybe it would be best if we could sit down, in full understanding of our altruistic frailty, and write one big check, once a year, to "the most efficient cause." But this is probably impossible. It is better if other people are always busy, bugging us to give more.

Many of us (though not I) like getting charitable mailings as a means of identifying new causes. Surely *somebody* responds to these mailings, otherwise they would not be sent. Believe it or not, some people try to get as much direct mail as possible; they read it for entertainment and edification.

But there is a cheaper way of connecting donors and charities, if only donors would cooperate.

It is very costly for the charity to search for the donor. To the charities we are but names, addresses, and of course zip codes. A giving donor is the proverbial needle in the haystack. It is easier and cheaper for the donor to look for the charity. We already have some idea of what causes we are interested in. So if we want to save charities money, we should go to them rather than making them look for us. Don't just wait for mailings. How about a Web search or the local public library? How about reading an advice columnist? Asking your friends? Write or e-mail your favorite author for his recommendations. I promise not to rent out your name and address to third-party brokers.

These calculations have an additional but very important implication. If we give only a small sum to a charity, and our name continues to be rented out, we are making charities in general worse off. Let me repeat that. If we give only a small sum to a charity, and our name continues to be rented out, we are making charities in general worse off. We would be harming the very groups we seek to help.

Are you giving away only $50 a year? *Don't let your address get onto those rented mailing lists.* If you are not going to restrict the renting of your name and address, I have a better suggestion. Don't send a check through the mail at all. Stuff some more cash in your pocket next time you are in Calcutta—or perhaps Cancun—and give it away on the street. Even without the tax break, we can do more good for the world this way.

The more devious lesson is that we can subvert the nonprofits we do not like. Are you offended by Ralph Nader, or perhaps you think PETA (People for the Ethical Treatment of Animals) goes too far? Does the Republican or Democratic National Committee make you angry? Run up their costs of operation.

Choose one nonprofit you do not like and send them twenty bucks. Once is enough. Mention that you are thinking of putting them in your will, or perhaps let it drop that you play at the local polo club or own a yacht. Keep your name on their mailing list. Send in all future changes of address. This action will drain that cause, and its like-minded allies, of hundreds or thousands of dollars for years to come.

• • •

SOME PLEAS DO not come in the mail but rather invade our TV screens and newspapers. We are literally deluged with requests for help.

For many of us the Asian tsunami of 2004 was an unprecedented event. Three hundred thousand people were killed by the water and the collateral damage, often with little more than a few minutes' notice. It is hard to imagine the terror they must have felt as they started running to higher ground. To make it worse, scientists knew a tidal wave was coming, but there was no established communications network for issuing a credible warning.

It is estimated that Americans sent at least $480 million (plus a governmental pledge of $350 million) to tsunami-related charities, most of it coming within a few months of the disaster. The global contribution is of course yet more, although I have not seen a comprehensive number for the total.

Few of us asked seriously whether this was the best charitable use of our funds. Most of us contributed as an emotional gut reaction. *Everyone* was giving. There was a celebrity concert and Michael Schumacher led the way by donating £7 million. My "highly intelligent and careful with money" wife gave to an office pool for tsunami-linked charities without looking twice at where the money would go and without asking me. Nor did I object when I heard. How could I bicker over marital procedure when so many poor, victimized Indonesians were living in shelters, awaiting fresh water and new lives?

Upon reflection the case for giving is not obvious. The stories of the victims are heart-rending, but extreme misery is not new to the world. Why didn't we send our money to Calcutta or to Haiti a few years earlier, or for that matter yesterday? For all their problems, many of the surviving tsunami victims had better lives in the reconstruction camps—and better future prospects—than do the very poorest people around the world.

Few Americans give to Haiti, in part, because the suffering of the country receives less publicity. A coup d'etat makes the news, especially if there is American involvement. We see on the screen how poor the Haitians are, but that is not the main framing of the story. Haiti has not had many specific and identifiable natural catastrophes. In fact, given its location in the Caribbean, the island has had surprisingly good luck with regard to hurricanes. Some Haitians credit the voodoo spirits for their fortune.

So why give to the tsunami victims but not the Haitians?

It could be argued that aid is more effective when many donors address a single disaster in a focused manner. The delivery of the aid might be easier or perhaps the aid can feed into a larger-scale effort. Yet the evidence is mixed. Much of the tsunami aid was squandered or could not find appropriate mechanisms of support. Much of the Katrina aid was lost due to corruption and mismanagement. The 9/11 aid often had no institutional support and literally no place to go. For instance, the Red Cross redirected more than $200 million donated for families of 9/11 victims to its own long-term goals and administrative costs. Concentrated aid is not necessarily more effective.

But to assess giving to disasters, we must switch from one side of the charitable sector to the other. Our look at Calcutta beggars and direct mail looked at the consequences of our giving for *the supply side of charity*; this included the costs incurred by beggars and charities. Now we should consider how our giving might affect *the demand to give to charity*.

I prefer a simple argument for giving to the tsunami victims. We should give to highly public causes because this motivates our peers to give more to those same causes.

To return to the central theme of scarcity, donors are frail in their altruism. Most of us mind a social gaffe more than a thousand deaths in China. Go to the Web and look up the infant mortality rate for Angola; according to the CIA it is 185 per 1,000 births, the highest such rate in the world. Yet few of us cry when we read this fact. Few of us will think about the same statistic tomorrow.

Remember EGYPTIAN FERRY SINKS IN RED SEA; 1,000 MAY BE LOST, from the February 4, 2006, *New York Times*? Did it change our lives? HUNDREDS FEARED DEAD IN CHINESE FLOODS made only page five of the *New York Times* (June 4, 2005).

Reports on the Holocaust, during World War II, could be found in many U.S. newspapers, but they did not make the headlines or even the first few pages. The newspapers thought that most people did not care very much. Maybe the newspaper editors did not care either. No public outrage had been circulating, and the newspapers apparently did not think they could create the outrage single-handedly. They let the stories lie. Yet we are mortified if we spill a drink on someone's dress at a cocktail party or make a stupid remark to the host. We would not think of walking into a public place in our pajamas. We feel very good if we have a clever anecdote at a social gathering.

We should take this facet of human nature and turn it to the advantage of charity.

When the public is interested in a charity, the attention feeds upon itself. Even if most supporters only pretend to care, they nonetheless will give money and time. Interest in the tragedy snowballs, often at very rapid rates. There is a "Cause of the Month." And when that cause is "in," it is very hot. Many of us care about being linked to the cause.

So once a snowball of charitable publicity starts rolling, support the trend. Bigger snowballs are more likely to gather force and spread to others. Malcolm Gladwell wrote of the "tipping point," by which a series of small actions add up to a large sequence of final effects. Most of our charity doesn't contribute to this kind of snowball effect, so when we have a chance to leverage our efforts, we should do so.

It may feel silly to partake in such an irrational process. But you don't have to be silly or irrational. Even if the cause-of-the-month mentality does not characterize solid, sober people like you, it does apply to many others. So we should hold our noses, join the cause, and talk up what is being done. This will induce more charity from others, especially from the trendy and the image-conscious but altruistically frail.

It is difficult to know how much the cause-of-the-month effect drives extra giving. But the data on 2005 are illustrative, especially since that year followed some major catastrophes. Relative to 2004 and adjusting for inflation, giving rose by 2.7 percent. Of that $15 billion total increase in giving, about half of it was directed at one of three major natural disasters: the tsunami, Gulf Coast hurricanes, and the earthquake in Pakistan. That same year, giving to the category of "social services" went up 28 percent, after three years of decline. Over half of that increase (16.7 percent) can be attributed to disaster relief.

The Inner Economist can recognize the rationale behind giving to the Cause of the Month. The forcing economic question again is: what is the relevant scarcity? In the case of charity, the answer is usually "people who give a damn." Yet in this case we can get people to care more, although they will not always respond for rational reasons or care out of true altruism.

Alternative approaches—which might uncharitably be attributed to a "bleeding heart"—focus on which victims are the most deserving. But this method, while it sounds caring, ignores the scarcity of true altruism. Instead we should try to find the most leveraged way of directing human attention to the problem of poverty. If we can influence other people, we should give to the tsunami victims or whatever else has become the current Cause of the Month; many of us will forget about being kind a day, week, or month later.

The economist goes further and asks about the proper extent of giving, or in economic language, the proper *margin*. If well-publicized causes create a snowball effect, why should we give to any *other* causes? Should we forget about Jerry Lewis and the March of Dimes? More tsunami aid still could have done more good. But no, don't hastily abandon other causes. Charitable addiction has real value. At some point the tsunami cause will disappear, no matter how great our initial dedication. Most of the tsunami victims—at least those who are still alive—have returned to some semblance of ordinary existence. If we give all our charity to the Cause of the Month, we will cut loose from our addictions to regular charitable causes. And once we stop giving to a charity, we are unlikely to resume. Fund-raisers know that we are, for better or worse, creatures of habit. If we have dropped our other charitable groups we may not pick them up again.

We should chase the charitable Cause of the Month with some of our giving but not all of it. We should not lose our connections with ongoing charitable causes. Some days the world does better than others, and there is not always a Cause of the Month. But in those quieter times we should still be giving something, to someone, somewhere, somehow.

So get addicted to your favorite causes, but also get addicted to the idea of chasing the Cause of The Month.

Given these arguments, let us revisit the question about the Calcutta beggars before moving on. Might you argue, drawing upon the logic of the tsunami case, that you should give to the beggars because otherwise you will forget about poverty altogether? Unlikely.

If anything, seeing large masses of beggars inures people to the idea of poverty. We come to expect poverty as a common problem and indeed as a hopeless cause. "How can we ever hope to lift all those beggars from poverty?" is a common question. We redefine the problem in terms we can handle, and that usually means ignoring it. The result is donor fatigue, not donor animation. The book and the movie *City of Joy* focused on the poor in Calcutta, but that Cause of the Month is over, if it ever got off the ground in the first place. So the Bengali beggars, I am sorry to say, do little for the overall charitable spirit. They are not about to become the new Cause of the Month.

If you want to get other people interested in giving, do not encourage more Calcutta beggars. They are far away and they are not receiving much media attention in the wealthier countries. More importantly, few other people are seeing you give money away in Calcutta. If you want to start such giving as a social trend, try writing about it instead.

• • •

WHEN IN DOUBT, let us measure. John A. List, an economist at the University of Chicago, has taken a close look at charities and especially donor behavior. List has worked as a part-time consultant for fund-raising campaigns and introduced deliberate variations into the fund-raising techniques and tabulated the results. He finds that donors are irrational in their giving, at least by the standards of an economist. For instance, donors do not respond to opportunities to receive something for nothing.

As we have seen, the "law of demand" is one of the most basic propositions about human behavior. As activities become cheaper, we do more of them. If the price of apples goes down, we buy more apples. Okay, maybe *you* don't buy more apples, but someone else will. It costs less to get an apple. What could be more straightforward?

But the complexities of human motivation can undercut or modify the law of demand, at least as economists usually imagine the law. If the price of helping other people falls, donors do not always give more. Oddly, donors could also give *less* and still help out as much as before, given the greater efficacy of a donation. But donors don't adjust in this way, either. Donor behavior exhibits a remarkable "stickiness": people tend to give set amounts, and they don't adjust much to changing circumstances. This suggests some combination of two possibilities. First, donors do not calculate very well. Second, donors do not care much about the people they are ostensibly trying to help.

Consider John List's experiments. It is well known that a "matching pledge"—if you give a dollar some other donor pledges to give a dollar more—boosts charitable contributions. Donors are enticed by the idea of "more bang for the buck." Yet the size of the match does not seem to matter. When some other donor pledges to give two or even three dollars to match outside contributions, we do not, in the aggregate, donate any more. List found this result after studying a database of over 50,000 prior donors.

This result is puzzling. If the match is 1 to 3, and our goal had been to get $800 in the hands of the charity, we must donate only $200. At the 1 to 1 match we had to donate $400 to achieve the same charitable end, which is clearly a more expensive proposition. Yet our altruistic instincts appear to be unmoved by the prospect of larger and more potent matching grants. The price of helping has fallen, yet the studied donors did not, in the aggregate, respond by helping more.

The most likely interpretation of these results is a bit cynical. Might it be that giving is often about affiliation rather than helping other people per se? We want to be a part of big and successful organizations. We want to be on winning sports teams, we want to work for successful companies, and we want to support the best and most influential charities. Being on the winning side makes us feel we are making a difference. Just think how most people—no matter how much cynicism they express about politics at the dinner table— would jump if they were invited for a session at the White House. Matching grants typically come from established and prestigious donors. After all, it takes a wealthy person or institution to promise to match any giving from others. Many donors seem to like the idea of undertaking a joint project with successful people or institutions. Having any match at all gives a stronger sense of affiliation with a worthy cause.

But a more potent match does not constitute a greater lure to give more. Despite what we tell ourselves, many donors are not so concerned with *how many* children will receive a diphtheria immunization. Did a $1,000 contribution lead to twenty, forty, or sixty immunizations? Well, that depends on the size of the match. Those are the details, and they are not the prime concern of the truly magnanimous donors.

"Great" donors focus on the nobility of the overall endeavor and the alliances they are building. Once those donors have the status of the affiliation with the match, it seems they stop thinking about the real purpose of charity.

"Seed money" also encourages people to give more to charities. Seed money refers to the practice of lining up major grants in advance, before announcing a "capital campaign" to raise a certain sum of money, often as high as $100 million or more. The seed money shows that prestigious and wealthy donors are already committed to the cause.

When the initial seed money is high, the subsequent fund-raising tends to go very well. One of List's experiments found that raising seed money from 10 to 67 percent leads to a nearly sixfold increase in subsequent contributions. Like a matching grant, seed money signals that the charity is part of a powerful and noble endeavor; the charity is the winning team, so to speak.

Charitable "refunds" have a positive but much smaller effect on giving. In another of List's studies, a policy of refunds boosted giving by only about 20 percent; this was much less effective than seed money. A refund means that if the charity does not reach its specified goal, donors get their money back. But most donors are not thrilled by the idea of refunds. They wish to believe that their cause is certain to succeed. Getting the refund would suggest that their initial donation was in fact a mistake. Why should a charity signal that it may be financially weaker, or perhaps less sound in execution, than donors want to believe? Winning teams—whether the New York Yankees or Michael Jordan's Chicago Bulls—are not in the habit of issuing refunds for poor performance. When I hear the word "refund," I think of a cheap department store or a radio that did not work.

List and his research team conducted another experiment on charitable giving. He and his research team conducted a door-to-door fund-raising experiment across nearly 5,000 households. The team experimented with a variety of methods, and of course some worked better than the others. They then measured the difference between the most effective method (in this context, selling lottery tickets) and the least effective method (just asking for money).

For purposes of contrast, List and the team tried another experiment. They increased the attractiveness of the woman who, on a door-to-door basis, asked for the money. The more attractive women (a "one standard deviation increase in attractiveness," in statistical terms) had as big a positive impact on giving as moving from the least successful fund-raising method to the most successful fund-raising method. This kind of distraction will only succeed, of course, if donors are not very focused on the final effects of their charitable giving.

In 2004, the Kellogg Foundation was criticized for spending $836,316 on a ten-day trip for nineteen donors to witness their poverty-alleviation programs in Africa by day while passing the evenings at a $1,000-per-night hunting lodge. The executive who ran the United Way for twenty-seven years pled guilty to embezzling about a half-million dollars. The CFO of the United Way later resigned, complaining that donation numbers had been fudged so that the chief executive could claim they were on the rise once again. More generally, many charities spend too much money on executive salaries, perks, and raising more money.

When a commercial business is that bad, it usually goes bankrupt fairly quickly. If the hamburger is too greasy, the service is too rude, or the prices are too high, consumers stop turning over money for the product. But these same mechanisms do not always keep bad charities in check.

Who feels good about giving to a group that spends its funds on plush carpets and expense accounts for the president? No one. But donors do not always scrutinize their charities very carefully or insist on measurable results. Many people become captive donors. They will dismiss any unfavorable information about the charity because they do not want to feel bad about their former giving. When our pride is at stake, we often don't look too closely at the truth. Remember self-deception? The result: many charities waste our money.

• • •

MANY CHARITABLE ACTIVITIES don't, in net terms, help anyone at all. For instance, an activity known as "charitable parachuting" is practiced in Scotland. A few Scottish doctors looked into the sport and its costs. Many novices are attracted to the activity, perhaps because it helps them feel they are working hard to save poor African babies. But the injury rate is high: 11 percent for minor injuries and 7 percent for serious injuries. Minor injuries cost the National Health Service £3,751 on average, and serious injuries cost £5,781 on average. The average parachutist raised only £30 for a day out.

Let's call it *negative charity*. Another example is training for weeks to run in charity races. If the race is a marathon, sometimes a few people die.

What about giving money to a church? Religious groups receive 40 to 60 percent of all personal donations in the United States; surely the crowd has some wisdom. But most of these donations keep churches going rather than finding their way to the poor. They pay for buildings and the salaries of clergy. Depending on your religious point of view, this *might* help the poor in the world to come. But if you want to help the poor in this world, give to a church that serves the poor, whether or not it is *your* church. If you insist on giving to your church, switch so that your new church has a poorer congregation.

The current fancy trend is to buy "fair trade" coffee. Fair trade sells a product at a premium price, under the premise that the workers are treated better and paid more, or at least paid more steadily. It sounds so nice. We get our fancy, exotic caffeine fix, usually doused with cream and dairy, in a tony atmosphere, while thinking Africa is no longer doomed. But will those purchases benefit the poor?

It depends. How about a product called "exploitation coffee"? You pay less, and they promise to treat the workers especially poorly. That wording is a less effective marketing ploy, but that is what the concept of fair trade boils down to. Whether we upgrade one option or downgrade the other is just semantics. A more neutral phrase would be neither "fair trade" nor "exploitation coffee," but rather, "quality differentiation." We can either have two classes of coffee (and workers), or one class of coffee (and workers). Splitting up the market into classes is good for the workers at the higher end, but it does not always help workers at the lower end. In fact it may hurt them. The jury remains out on this idea. Would you buy a product called "quality differentiation" coffee? Maybe not.

Nicholas Kristof, a reporter at the *New York Times*, had a novel idea for how to reduce suffering. He got on a plane to Cambodia and decided to buy and free two slaves. It cost him $150 and $203, respectively, to free each slave, plus of course plane fare and expenses. The girls were, most likely, otherwise destined to lives of prostitution, rape, and quite possibly AIDS. A number of charities have been buying and freeing slaves in Sudan.

These activities sound virtuous, but there is a danger: if we buy out slaves, we bid up the price of slaves. In turn more victims will be enslaved. (Handgun purchase plans, a common idea for cleaning up inner cities, encounter a similar problem, as do repurchase programs for high-emissions automobiles.) Kristof's two purchases were probably too small to affect the overall market for slaves or to push up the price. But if many of us started doing the same thing (might someone try to sell the freedom of slaves on eBay?), the price would rise. Slavery, and the accompanying capture and oppression, might become a bigger problem. A given person might stay a slave for a shorter period of time, but more people would circulate into slavery for a while.

This problem is not a new one. For a long time economists have debated the best way to use speculation to discourage the development of a market. The answer is counterintuitive, but it makes sense upon consideration: *buy up a great deal of the item*. When other sellers are ready to take their profits, *dump the entire stock on the market at once, thereby lowering the price*. Other market players will not receive much, if any, profit. Once the existence of this strategy becomes known, the market will wither rather than flourish.

No, I am not suggesting that we buy stocks of slaves and hold them for later sale. But in many circumstances it is this strategy—not buying slaves to free them—that will discourage enslavement. Buying the freedom of slaves may end up as counterproductive, so we should search further for good ideas.

· · ·

WE SHOULD LOOK elsewhere to help others, yes, but we should not look to tipping service help as a means of feeling good about ourselves. Tipping is a relatively wasteful means of helping other people. Furthermore, tipping makes us feel virtuous and charitable and thus may substitute for real benevolence to the truly needy.

I tried a simple experiment. I had eaten at my favorite local Vietnamese Pho noodle soup joint. If you ever have visited a Pho restaurant, you will know that the customer pays by going up to the cashier, where the bill is waiting (though sometimes they can't believe that the white guy ordered the soup with the tripe).

I had my change and I was going to leave the tip. But I thought that perhaps an experiment was in order: why not leave the tip on *another* table, served by the same waiter, rather than on my table? So for just a moment, I put the money down on the other table. I knew the same waiter would receive it. But upon a very brief reflection I recoiled in horror and quickly grabbed the money back. That waiter would think I stiffed him. He would think badly of *me*.

I realized I don't care how much the waiter gets. But I *did* wish—strongly—to uphold my side of the dining bargain. Leaving money on the other table doesn't meet that end. I left the money on my table and threw down a few extra quarters to relieve my mental tension. It felt like a close call, as if I had almost wandered out of Nordstrom without paying for the new shirt in my hand.

An opportunity to tip has some elements of extortion. The service provider comes along. He is, if trained well, not in the slightest pushy or demanding. We imagine ourselves being served by a gracious butler with white gloves and a British BBC accent. Or perhaps our waitress is a cute Midwestern girl with curly hair and a big smile. She would like to go to college once she saves up a little money.

We respond to these situations. Because of cultural expectations, we know we are expected to tip. There is an implicit exchange. We give money to the waiter. He is especially friendly as we walk out the door: "Thank *you*. Have a GREAT evening." The exchange reaffirms our sense of ourselves as WORTHY AND GENEROUS PEOPLE WHO REWARD QUALITY. If it is a waitress, perhaps we will get lucky. She might touch us on the back.

I am not against the practice of tipping, any more than I am against hiring a piano teacher or hiring help to mow the lawn. But as a means of helping the world, tipping falls flat. The tips are received by people who already have jobs. Most tipping occurs in relatively wealthy countries. Many of the young workers who receive tips have low current income but high prospects in life. They have so many years ahead of them: marriage, kids, new puppies, lots of sex, and plenty of new movies and TV shows to watch. Maybe they won't all be millionaires, but why are we helping *them* out?

Here's one final point, direct from the toolbox of the economist. Let's say *everyone* tipped 25 rather than 15 percent. What would happen? The market for waiters is competitive, and most waiters are paid what they are worth, no more or no less. If customers pay waiters more, employers will get away with paying them less. Waiters won't receive more money, but restaurant owners will, and at the expense of diners. Is that the kind of altruism we had in mind?

If you wish to use tipping to help the poor, start by tipping less. Don't let tipping build up your favorable self-image or become a substitute for charity. Stick to 15 percent, even when the waitress is cute, touches you, or wears a flower in her hair. Send the rest of the money abroad. You'll also be saving waitresses some effort. We don't want them to end up like the Calcutta beggar who spends money and resources trying to get . . . more money and resources.

• • •

IF TIPS ARE not a worthy form of charity, what about gifts to your friends and loved ones? I suspect many readers, having read the chapter on how to look good, already know the answer.

The *Financial Times* reported the story of one Karen Davis, who started a hickory-baked ham company in Georgia in 1979. Over the next twenty years, she received 400 to 500 different gifts in the form or shape of a pig. We should not conclude, as some economists have done, that gift-giving is wasteful. Gift-giving is fun, or at least it can be. But it is not the best means of helping other people.

Economist Joel Waldfogel, mentioned at the beginning of this chapter, has tried to estimate how much gifts are worth to the recipient. He found that most of us do not value the gifts we receive in proportion to what was spent. In percentage terms, if we exclude cash gifts, Waldfogel found that people value their gifts at 83.9 percent of their cost. This figure was derived from a survey, and frankly I think most of the respondents were lying. I would be surprised if the true average valuation was 40 percent of what was spent. But if we take Waldfogel's very conservative estimate as given, the "deadweight loss" of gift-giving runs to at least $4 billion a year. That number attempts to express the difference between what was spent and how much value was received.

Many gifts are clunkers, whether it be that onyx paperweight or the doggie sweater that doesn't fit. Even if our friends can guess what we might want, they often don't know what we already have. A Harris Interactive survey showed that half of American adults admit to "re-gifting." Seventy-eight percent of those polled felt that re-gifting was acceptable at least some of the time. Four percent admitted that they re-gifted not because of what they received, but because they disliked the giver.

The least effective gift-givers appear to be the elderly. The value of their gifts to the recipients is less than half of the money they spend. Many of the elderly don't have any idea what interests their grandchildren. So if you are old, give cash if you don't already. Waldfogel found that aunts and uncles were also poorly qualified to judge the utility of a gift. These loss estimates fail to account for the time spent buying gifts, which can run many hours.

The point is not to attack gift-giving, which is a marvelous institution. But it is a self-centered institution; it is not about saving the world.

Let's say you give your sister soccer tickets for $100, but she values them at only $50. There is a loss of $50 on her side, but by no means is the offering simply a mistake. After all, maybe you *enjoyed* giving her the tickets. You received a thrill imagining your sister at the soccer game. For weeks you looked forward to seeing her open the ticket envelope. You can savor the look on her face for months or even years to come. How much pleasure did you get from helping out your sister? Well, probably your pleasure exceeded $100 in value— or at least you expected it would—because that is how much money you spent on the tickets.

So let us go back and calculate the total value of the gift-giving experience. Your sister gained $50 of value. You gained $100 or more of pleasure. Total gain: $150. Total cost: $100. That is a good deal: how many mutual funds will yield a 50 percent return over such a short period of time? The numbers will vary with the details of the example, but it is easy to see why gift-giving continues.

But notice that the selfish gains of the giver are required to create the net value from the gift. If we take away the joy of giving, the gift does not make the world a better place. So we have two simple rules: 1) presents are wonderful and so is the institution of present-giving, and 2) presents are a lousy way to help other people.

Of course we give presents for many reasons. I was being generous when I assumed that we give out of the joy of our hearts. Many people give just out of show. They want to signal they are rich, show they have access to wonderful gifts ("how *did* you get those tickets?"), or impress other family members. I have seen gifts based on hostility. A man might give his wife a long and complex novel for her birthday, in part to show he resents her attachment to the television set. If one person is showing off and demonstrating resentment by giving gifts, other people in the room may feel inadequate or underappreciated. This is not helping the world.

Other times we give gifts to control people. The gift is not a gift at all. The gift is a signal that if the other person does us favors, he or she can expect more payment in the future. B. Douglas Bernheim, Andrei Shleifer, and Larry Summers conducted a comprehensive study of parental bequests; the paper was titled "The Strategic Bequest Motive." The results will not surprise any reader of Ben Jonson's *Volpone*, in which toadies curry favor with a nobleman to receive a large inheritance. In modern America, the more children called or visited their parents, the more likely they received a significant bequest. Those results are adjusting for the wealth of the parents, thus isolating the effect of greater attention on the size of the final gift. Both the children and the parents are behaving selfishly rather than showing unconditional love.

Why not just give cash? It is more common than ever before to give cash gifts at weddings. The practice of "the register" is not the same as getting the cash, but it does ensure people don't give us useless junk. Cash gifts have long been standard practice for Bar Mitz-vahs. Often the intent is that the money helps pay for a college educa-tion. Nonetheless, in another context, if you give your sister $50 for her birthday, she will probably feel insulted. She would rather be taken to a $50 dinner, even if she would not have spent so much of her own money on food. The meal "feels right" as a gift, but the money does not.

It is not obvious why cash gifts are often (but not always) consid-ered to be in bad taste. Perhaps gift-giving is an exercise in showing we understand our loved ones. Like other forms of signaling, giving pres-ents puts us through a test. Our loved ones see how much we are in touch with what they want. *Anyone* can use a gift of cash. But how many men can pick out just the right kind of flowers or bring just the right bottle of wine for a romantic evening?

Giving cash shows, at most, that we are good at earning money. But few people wish to admit that money is a relevant criterion for how they choose their friends. At the same time, if we need to carry thou-sands of dollars of value to a Bar Mitzvah, cash or long-term invest-ments are the only sensible options.

When small sums are at stake, very smart or very sensitive people should be able to give gifts of *greater* value than cash. CDs cost $17.99 or so, but a wonderful CD is worth more than $100 to me. A person who can pick out the right CD does me a greater service than just giv-ing me the money. But that CD is very hard for most people to identify. Again, gift-giving signals both personal attachment and individual skill. If you and I keep on giving gifts to each other, it suggests we are able to exchange some truly delightful benefits. But we are moving away from the idea of charity.

Most of all, we should be suspicious of people who seek gifts. Tom Locke went on a one-man crusade to receive as many gifts as possible from corporate America. He wrote many letters, such as this one:

Dear Sir or Madam:

You may love to see me smile, but I, however, love to see me eat. Please send me coupons for free McDonald's products, so that I may continue to eat (and smile). Thank you well in advance,

Tom Locke, eating enthusiast

CVS, the drugstore company, got this:

Dear Sir or Madam:

I am a health and wellness addict. Please send me a random product which you think I would enjoy. It doesn't have to be something big, just something nice! I like surprises. Thank you in advance,

Tom Locke, health enthusiast

Locke sent one hundred letters in similar formats to leading American consumer product corporations. Many responded with free products, but Wrigley's had the right idea. They told him to go buy his own gum. Smucker's just said "no."

By the way, many people feel a need to be appreciated. Research indicates that experiences are remembered for longer than possessions. Give concert tickets rather than a compact disc. Give your son or daughter a trip abroad rather than money toward a car.

• • •

AND NOW FOR what is proving to be a revolutionary idea in improving the lives of the world's poor. How about we lend out our money instead of giving it away? Counterintuitively, it has been suggested that we should abandon the role of charity angel for that of moneylender. Daniel Akst, writing for Slate.com, refers to micro-credit as "the best way to spend a little money helping the world's poorest citizens."

Micro-credit is the practice of giving very small loans—often no more than $100—to the world's poor. Millions of people around the globe use micro-credit to set up small businesses or sometimes just to pay their medical bills. Micro-credit is particularly well-known for helping women set up tailoring shops or small retail outlets in their communities.

The micro-credit revolution started in 1976, when an economics professor, one Muhammad Yunus, started the Grameen Bank Project in Bangladesh. Here is someone who gave something very good indeed to the world. In 2006 his efforts won Yunus the Nobel Peace Prize. *Grameen,* by the way, is the Bengali word for "rural." Yunus was convinced that it is possible to lend money to the poor, even without collateral. Often the loans are made to small groups of five or ten people, and the lender uses mutual liability and peer pressure to ensure repayment. If the neighbor does not pay, each group member is responsible. Many micro-credit projects have repayment rates as high as 98 percent. Groups that repay their loans are eligible for larger borrowings the next time around.

Often micro-credit funds come from charities, from governments, or from multilateral agencies such as the World Bank. But private commercial banks are taking a growing interest in micro-lending for profit. As economic growth spreads around the world, banks are realizing that many individual borrowing needs are quite small. Furthermore, today's micro-borrower may be tomorrow's depositor.

We can see why micro-credit might do more good than charity. The new small businesses feed into the local economy. The business owners develop lasting skills. The need to repay the loan—regular payments are often required as frequently as weekly—enforces discipline and work. On top of everything else, donating to a micro-credit charity keeps much of the original capital intact for continued lending. There is a chance the donation will lead to self-sustaining profit and many years of assistance.

Micro-credit also helps solve problems within families. When we *give away* money to the entrepreneurial poor, their friends, relatives, or members of their kinship networks often come looking for a cut of the proceeds. Given that many of these societies operate on a strong familial and communal basis, it can be difficult to say no. The result is dissolution of the funds and a scattering of potential impact. The funds end up spent rather than invested. But when the money is lent out and repayments are required on a frequent basis, the entrepreneurial borrowers find it easier to keep their relatives at bay.

Of course micro-credit can misfire. Many people would start new businesses in any case. They use their micro-credit loans to support lazy relatives. Some individuals borrow from the micro-lenders at a low interest rate and then use that money as collateral to borrow even more from extortionate local lenders at a much higher rate. The money is spent on a television set and the result is perpetual indebtedness and greater desperation, not a new enterprise.

In Hyderabad, India, economists are studying how micro-credit changes people's lives. An Indian company named Spandana has started extending micro-credit to thousands of lower-middle-class borrowers in the city slums. But not everyone has access to these loans. Two years later, a follow-up survey will look at just how big a difference micro-credit has made. Are family incomes higher? How many new businesses have been started where micro-credit is available? Has the status of women improved?

We await the final results, but this economist is hopeful. I visited these micro-credit markets in Hyderabad and met many eager, responsible, and entrepreneurial Indian women. None of them had chopped off their limbs in search of sympathy and larger donations. In an interview, I asked the Spandana CEO, Padmaja Reddy, how she could be sure that the company was doing the world good. Her answer was simply that the women keep repaying the old loans and coming back for new loans. It might be said that these women are discovering their Inner Economists.

Either way, there is a new micro-credit system that doesn't require you to journey as far as I did. Now, you can make your loan over the Internet. Here is a report from the (North American) blogger Cornelius:

> I feel good. I just lent $25 to Christopher Odeke. He's a taxi driver from Bukedea, Uganda, and needs $1200 to buy a new engine for his van.
>
> I've signed up to Kiva.org, a service that lists entrepreneurs from developing countries who need small amounts of money and lets anyone get personally involved in helping them out. The site provides a journal where the borrowers can describe how their business is doing and lenders can make comments.

Kiva means "agreement" or "unity" in Swahili. You can lend as little as $25, Paypal.com will process your loan for free, and you'll get e-mails on the progress of the business you are funding.

Ten years from now, will Kiva still be going strong? I don't know. Will there be other new and innovative ways to fight poverty? For sure.

10

Your Inner Economist and the Future of Civilization

THE SUGGESTIONS IN the last chapter for helping other people culminated in one simple but powerful idea: help other people by first helping yourself, by first fulfilling your own potential. I think of this entire book as a guide to helping yourself in a socially responsible manner and thus as a guide to helping other people.

Your Inner Economist understands incentives but also understands that human values are needed to make markets work smoothly.

When markets and human values work together, the gains are immense. The market economy and capitalism are among the greatest enablers of civilization. Our lives are comfortable instead of wracked with hard physical labor, chronic malnutrition, and massive losses of women and babies during childbirth, to cite just a few features of earlier times. Whether our political views are right-wing, left-wing, or elsewhere on the spectrum, we can agree on these facts.

Imagine a time traveler from the eighteenth century visiting the life of Bill Gates. He would witness television, automobiles, refrigerators, central heating, antibiotics, plentiful food, flush toilets, cell phones, personal computers, and affordable air travel, among other remarkable benefits. But the most impressive features of Gates's life, from a historical point of view, are shared by most middle-class Americans today.

Markets are not just about the steam engine, iron foundries, or today's silicon-chip factories. Markets also supported Shakespeare, Haydn, and the modern book superstore. The rise of oil painting, classical music, and print culture were all part of the same broad social and economic developments, namely the rise of capitalism, modern technology, rule of law, and consumer society. The Renaissance occurred when growing cities and reopened trade routes created enough wealth to stimulate demand for beautiful art. Beethoven gave music lessons and concerts to a rising middle class and later sold them sheet music; his rise required the printing press, the affordable piano, and ready travel around Europe.

Markets, of course, also have their uglier side. In Bangalore, India, the nurse often takes away the newborn baby, returning it only when the parents pay a bribe; the price is $12 for a baby boy, $7 for a baby girl. A 1999 survey reported that nine of ten families giving birth in the hospitals had to pay such bribes. There are also reports of bribes to have the baby delivered, to get the newborn immunized, or to obtain supposedly "free" medicines.

During one riot in Michigan, one woman sold stones to rioters. According to police, she used the money to pay her cable television bill. Small stones went for $1, larger stones brought in $5 a piece. Most of the rocks were thrown at the police. There is a sick poetic justice in the story. The woman claimed that she collected about $70 from her efforts, but she stopped when she was hit by a rock herself.

There is worse.

A bribe of a thousand rubles—about $34 at the time—sufficed for an airline agent to admit a Chechen on board a Russian plane just before takeoff. The agent pocketed the money and on a ticket the

Chechen held for another flight she wrote "Admit on board Flight 1047." The woman blew up the plane. Or recall that Chechen gunmen seized a Moscow theater in 2002, leading later to the deaths of 129 hostages. The terrorists had paid off police to be allowed to transport a small armory of weapons into Moscow.

Bribing police and security forces is not a path toward a glorious future.

The West has succeeded as much as it has because it embraced the values of self-criticism, individual rights, science, and the idea that government is the servant of the people, not vice versa. Corruption, however much it continues, is regarded as outrageous rather than inevitable. We should not take these values for granted. Nor will every instance of a market support these values. The former Soviet Union tried to move to a market economy yet without the underlying cultural foundations. While Russian citizens are better off than in times past, the result has been a collapse in the social fabric and a partial return to tyranny.

The future of our civilization is based on prudence, critical self-reflection, belief in higher values, and wisdom in matters of ordinary, everyday life. It is not about grabbing as much as possible, as quickly as possible. Just as culture often relies on markets, so do markets require cultural foundations. Your Inner Economist is a source of practical advice, but in the bigger picture your Inner Economist helps support social order. On the surface this is a book about our lives, but in its undercurrents it is also about sustaining and extending a free society.

So go ahead, use that Inner Economist to do better for yourself, your friends, and your family. Society depends on it.

References

Chapter 2

For the Camerer Davos survey, one citation is from www.stnews.org/altruism-3792.htm, *Science and Theology News*, online edition. The study about the tidy students, and related examples, are covered in *The Age of Propaganda*, by Anthony Pratkanis and Elliot Aronson, New York: Owl Books, 2001.

The study on parking tickets is by Raymond Fisman and Eduard Miguel, "Cultures of Corruption: Evidence from U.N. Parking Tickets," National Bureau of Economic Research working paper #12312, June 2006. For the reports on Chad, see http://www.travel-island.com/interesting.places/chad.html, and http://www.washingtonpost.com/wp-dyn/content/article/2006/04/13/AR2006041301897.html. On disability in Norway I have drawn on this *New York Times* story, among other sources: http://select.nytimes.com/search/restricted/article?res=F40B14FE3F590C768EDDAE0894DC404482.

For a survey of the research on when financial incentives are effective, see Colin F. Camerer and Robin M. Hogarth, "The Effects of Financial Incentives in Experiments: A Review and Capital-Labor-Production Framework," *Journal of Risk and Uncertainty*, 1999, 19:1–3, 7–42. Another relevant piece is Sarah E. Bonner, Reid Hastie, Geoffrey B. Sprinkle, and S. Mark Young, "A Review of the Effects of Financial Incentives on Performance in Laboratory Tasks: Implications for Management Accounting," *Journal of Management Accounting Research,* 2000, 12, 19–64.

On the distinction between intrinsic and extrinsic motivations, I have been influenced by Bruno Frey, *Not Just for the Money,* Cheltenham: Edward Elgar Publishing, 1997, and Alfie Kohn, *Punished by Rewards: The Trouble with Gold Stars, Incentive Plans, A's Praise, and Other Bribes,* Boston: Houghton Mifflin, 1995, among other sources.

On how high prizes and task importance can induce groupthink, see Robert S. Baron, Joseph A. Vandello, and Bethany Brunsman, "The Forgotten Variables in Conformity Research: Impact of Task Importance on Social Influence," *Journal of Personality and Social Psychology,* 1996, 71, 5, 915–927.

On the tendency for individuals to respond badly to incentives when they perceive a lack of control, see Edward L. Deci, Richard Koestner, and Richard M. Ryan, "A Meta-Analytic Review of Experiments Examining the Effects of Extrinsic Rewards on Intrinsic Motivation," *Psychological Bulletin,* 1999, 125, 6, 627–668. See also Sharon S. Brehm and Jack W. Brehm, *Psychological Reactance: A Theory of Freedom and Control,* New York: Academic Press, 1981.

On how bonuses boost performance when they signal competence at a task, see Edward L. Deci, "Applications of Research on the Effects of Rewards," in *The Hidden Costs of Reward: New Perspectives on the Psychology of Human Motivation,* edited by Mark R. Lepper and David Greene, Hillsdale, New Jersey: Lawrence Erlbaum Associates, 1978, pp. 193–203.

On the problems with paying for grades, see John Condry, "The Role of Incentives in Socialization," in *The Hidden Costs of Reward: New Perspectives on the Psychology of Human Motivation,* edited by Mark R. Lepper and David Greene, Hillsdale, New Jersey: Lawrence Erlbaum Associates, 1978, pp. 179–192.

On the endurance of pain, see Sharon L. Baker and Irving Kirsch, "Cognitive Mediators of Pain Perception and Tolerance," *Journal of Personality and Social Psychology,* 1991, 61, 3, 504–510. On trying too hard, see for instance Hal R. Arkes, Robyn M. Dawes, and Caryn Christensen, "Factors influencing the use of a decision rule in a probabilistic task," *Organizational Behavior and Human Decision Processes,* 1986, 37, 93–110.

Chapter 3

On peer effects and drinking, see the work of H. Wesley Perkins, such as "Misperceiving the College Drinking Norm and Related Problems: A Nationwide Study of Exposure to Prevention Information, Perceived Norms and Student Alcohol Misuse," *Journal of Studies on Alcohol,* July 2005, 470–478.

For Randall Parker on meetings, see his blog Futurepundit.com, http://www.futurepundit.com/archives/001913.html#001913NetscapeMarkup\Shell\Open\Command.

For the surveys on meetings and their costs, see Roger K. Mosvick and Robert B. Nelson, *We've Got to Stop Meeting Like This!* Indianapolis: Park Avenue Productions, revised edition, 1996.

On Roland Fryer, I have drawn upon two blog posts by my co-blogger Alex Tabarrok and the sources cited therein; see http://www.marginalrevolution.com/marginalrevolution/2005/11/paying_for_perf.html, and http://www.marginalrevolution.com/marginalrevolution/2004/12/milton_friedman.html.

The estimate of the costs of lateness is from an article from *The Economist,* "The Price of Lateness," November 3, 2003, online at http://www.economist.com/displayStory.cfm?story_id=2238214. Alex Tabarrok brought this piece to my attention. Some blog posts on the topic are here: http://www.marginalrevolution.com/marginalrevolution/2003/11/how_to_change_s.html and here: http://www.marginalrevolution.com/marginalrevolution/2004/03/punctuality.html.

On declining RSVP rates, see my earlier blog post: http://www.marginalrevolution.com/marginalrevolution/2004/02/why_rsvp.html.

A MarginalRevolution.com reader, Robert Ayres, suggested to me the idea of entering the salary of everyone at the meeting into a computer.

Chapter 4

On what is sold from hotel rooms, see *Forbes,* June 7 issue, 2004, p. 124. On museum admissions not covering the costs of visitors, the American Association of Museums has published a financial information survey, *2003 Museum Financial Information*; a summary press release is at: https://69.63.132.61/pressreleases.cfm?mode=list&id=54.

James Twitchell's material on overexposed artworks is from his *Branded*

Nation: The Marketing of Megachurch, College Inc., and Museumworld, New York: Simon and Schuster, 2005.

For why some pictures sell for more than others, see "Why Some Pictures Go for More Than Others," in the May 2004 issue of *The Art Newspaper.* http://www.marginalrevolution.com/marginalrevolution/2004/05/what_make s_a_pa.html.

The Harold Bloom quotation is from his *How to Read and Why.* New York: Scribner, 2001.

The Jerrold Jenkins estimate is oft-repeated, but I cannot track down how much it is based in fact. It should not be taken very literally or as more than one person's guess. But see http://parapublishing.com/sites/para/resources/ statistics.cfm, and http://www.google.com/search?hl=en&lr=&q=jenkins+ group+books+%22never+reads+another+book%22&btnG=Search.

On why people buy and carry around books, see *The Guardian,* October 24, 2005, http://books.guardian.co.uk/news/articles/0,6109,1599060,00.html.

A variety of humorous Amazon.com reviews can be found here: http:// www.themorningnews.org/archives/reviews/lone_star_statements.php.

For a look at musical studies on heavy metal, the taste of cosmopolitan- ites, and low-status genres, see Bethany Bryson, "Anything but Heavy Metal": Symbolic Exclusion and Musical Dislikes," *American Sociological Review,* 2006, 61, 5, 884–899.

On the music lists of best-selling artists and groups, here is one source: http://www.2blowhards.com/archives/001550.html#001550.

Chapter 5

For the property monologue, see http://www.mises.org/story/2058. The citation to Dr. Rangel can be found here: http://www.marginalrevolution .com/marginalrevolution/2003/12/impressing_a_wo.html.

Richard Harter's game-theoretic approach to the toilet-seat problem can be found here: http://www.scq.ubc.ca/?p=108. That is published in *The Science Creative Quarterly,* September/November 2006, 2.

On pickup lines, the paper is here: http://www.sciencedirect.com/ science?_ob=ArticleURL&_udi=B6V9F-4HC76VB-1&_coverDate=03%2F31 %2F2006&_alid=366110572&_rdoc=1&_fmt=&_orig=search&_qd=1&_cdi =5897&_sort=d&view=c&_acct=C000035118&_version=1&_urlVersion=0 &_userid=650615&md5=41c72be12383dc18082f57c8f8f6d5ec. "Chat-Up

Lines as Male Sexual Displays," by Christopher Bale, Rory Morrison, and Peter G. Caryl, in *Personality and Individual Differences*, March 2006, 40, 4, 655–664.

Here is a link to some reports on Nur Malena Hassan: http://www .marginalrevolution.com/marginalrevolution/2004/09/de_gustibus.html.

The Bryan Caplan quotation on Robin Hanson is at: http://econlog .econlib.org/archives/2005/03/robin_radon_and.html.

For Prudie on the wedding, see http://www.slate.com/id/2102755/.

Here is Megan's ad: http://fromthearchives.blogspot.com/2006/07/ beyond-parody_08.html. You will find her reasoning here: http://fromthearchives .blogspot.com/2006/07/i-would-change-it-but-im-already-tired.html and here: http://fromthearchives.blogspot.com/2006/07/second-degree.html.

On how torture tries to completely break down a person's sense of control over his environment, see Alfred W. McCoy, *A Question of Torture: CIA Interrogation, from the Cold War to the War on Terror*, New York: Metropolitian Books, 2006, chapter 3. On successful resistance to torture, see that same book, p. 204. On American POWs in Vietnam, see Stuart I. Rochester and Frederick Kiley, *Honor Bound: American Prisoners of War in Southeast Asia, 1961–1973*, Annapolis: Naval Institute Press, 1998, chapter eight. On American experiences in resisting torture in Somalia, see Michael J. Durant, *In the Company of Heroes*, New York: G.P. Putnam's Sons, pp. 92, 102–105, 2003.

On Mark Frank, see http://www.buffalo.edu/news/fast-execute.cgi/ article-page.html?article=7930009. The quotations of Bella DePaulo and Maureen O'Sullivan are from *Science News Online*, July 31, 2004, vol. 166, no. 5, "Deception Detection: Psychologists Try to Learn How to Spot a Liar." A good survey of what we know about lying is "Suspects, Lies and Videotape: An Analysis of Authentic High-Stake Liars," *Law and Human Behavior*, June 2002, 26, 3, 365–376. For a look at how often people lie, and a good general survey of our knowledge of lying, see Aldert Vrij, *Detecting Lies and Deceit: The Psychology and Lying and the Implications for Professional Practice*, New York: John Wiley & Sons, 2000. The new technology for "monitoring your date" was written up in Nature.com, http://www.nature.com/news/2005/050314/full/050314-14.html, published on March 17, 2005, "Utensils Divulge Dinner Date's Feelings," by Roxanne Khamsi. On brain scans and eye scans, see Jeffrey Kluger, "How to Spot a Liar," *Time*, Sunday, August 2006, on the Web at http://www.time.com/ time/magazine/printout/0.8816.1229109.00.html.

The Rick Harbaugh and Theodore To paper is "False Modesty: When

Disclosing Good News Looks Bad," January 2006 version, available at http://www.bus.indiana.edu/riharbau/FalseModesty.pdf.

Chapter 6

I have drawn the idea of building frustrations from conversations with my colleague, Robin Hanson.

On the advantages of self-deception for romantic love, see in particular the work of Sandra L. Murray, such as "The Quest for Conviction: Motivated Cognition in Romantic Relationships," *Psychological Inquiry*, 1999, 10, 1, 23–34, or Sandra L. Murray, John G. Holmes, and Dale W. Griffin, "The Benefits of Positive Illusions: Idealization and the Construction of Satisfaction in Close Relationships," *Journal of Personality and Social Psychology*, 1996, 70, 1, 79–98, or Sandra L. Murray, John G. Holmes, Dan Daolderman, and Dale W. Griffin, "What the Motivated Mind Sees: Comparing Friends' Perspectives to Married Partners' Views of Each Other," *Journal of Experimental Social Psychology*, 2000, 36, 600–620. See also the work of Norm O'Rourke and Phillipe Cappeliez, such as "Marital Satisfaction and Self-Deception: Reconstruction of Relationship Histories Among Older Adults," *Social Behavior and Personality*, 2005, 33, 3, 273–282.

On the polls of various people thinking they are above average, see Thomas Gilovich, *How We Know What Isn't So*, New York: Free Press, 1991, p. 77. On the sociologists, see Frank R. Westie, "Academic Expectations of Professional Immortality: A Study of Legitimation," *The American Sociologist*, February 1973, 8, 19–32. On thinking that one's driving is above average, see "Are We All Less Risky and More Skillful Than Our Fellow Drivers?" *Acta Psychologica*, 1981, 47, 143–148. On criticizing one's previous self, see Anne E. Wilson and Michael Ross, "From Chump to Champ: People's Appraisals of Their Earlier and Present Selves," *Journal of Personality and Social Psychology*, 2001, 80, 4, 572–584. A good general introduction to the self-deception topic is Eduardo Giannetti's *Lies We Live By: The Art of Self-Deception*, London: Bloomsbury, 2001.

For good surveys of the research on self-deception, and overrating one's talents and personal qualities, see Justin Kruger and David Dunning, "Unskilled and Unaware of It: How Difficulties in Recognizing One's Own Incompetence Lead to Inflated Self-Assessments," *Journal of Personality and Social Psychology*, December 1999, 77, 6, 1121–1134. Another useful piece is Shelley E. Taylor and Jonathan D. Brown, "Illusion and Well-Being: A Social Psychological Perspective on Mental Health," *Psychological Bulletin*, 1988, 105, 2, 195–210.

For experimental evidence that people are more likely to think their claims are just, see James Konow, "Fair Shares: Accountability and Cognitive Dissonance in Allocation Decisions," *American Economic Review*, September 2000, 90, 4, 1072–1091. For the study of gym membership, see Stefano DellaVigna and Ulrike Malmendier, "Paying Not to Go to the Gym," *American Economic Review*, June 2006, 96, 3, 694–719.

On the unwillingness of people to defer to experts, and what that means, see my paper with Robin Hanson, "Are Disagreements Honest?" at http://hanson.gmu.edu/deceive.pdf#search=%22hanson%20cowen%20most%20disagreements%20honest%22.

On the likelihood that the depressed self-deceive much less, see Delroy L. Paulhus, "Self-Deception and Impression Management in Test Responses," in *Personality Assessment via Questionnaires: Current Issues in Theory and Measurement*, edited by A. Angleitner and J.S. Wiggins, Berlin: Springer-Verlag, 1986, 143–165.

On 9/11 plots, see for instance Erica Goode, "Finding Answers in Secret Plots," *The New York Times*, Sunday, March 10, 2002, WK3.

For some observations on UFOs, see Douglas Kern, "Internet Killed the Alien Star," at http://www.techcentralstation.com/110905A.html, accessed October 16, 2006.

The Prudie column can be found on Slate.com, here: http://www.slate.com/id/2134915/.

The Web site on celebrity tippers can be found here: http://www.stainedapron.com/celebs.htm, accessed on October 2, 2006.

On overspending, I have drawn on "The Shopping Momentum Effect," by Ravi Dhar, Joel Huber, and Uzma Khan, at http://cci.som.yale.edu/docs/Shopping_Momentum.2004.pdf, accessed October 16, 2006; also forthcoming in the *Journal of Marketing Research*.

On the loss of productivity in groups, the meta-study referred to is M. Diehl and W. Stroebe, "Productivity Loss in Brainstorming Groups: Toward the Solution of a Riddle," *Journal of Personality and Social Psychology*, 1987, 53, 497–509. A similar conclusion is found by B. Mullen, C. Johnson, and E. Salas, "Productivity Loss in Brainstorming Groups: A Meta-Analytic Integration," *Basic and Applied Social Psychology*, 1991, 12, 3–24. On the 80 percent who think group brainstorming is better, see Bernard A.

Nijstad, Wolfgang Stroebe, and Hein F.M. Lodewijkx, "The Illusion of Group Productivity: A Reduction of Failures Explanation," *European Journal of Social Psychology*, 2006, 36, 31–48. That paper also considers the evidence on the costs of making people wait their turn before speaking. See also Bernard A. Nijstad, Wolfgang Stroebe, and Hein F.M. Lodewijkx, "Production Blocking and Idea Generation: Does Blocking Interfere with Cognitive Processes?," *Journal of Experimental Social Psychology*, 2003, 39, 531–548.

For Alex Tabarrok's account of why he welcomes my advice to calculate probabilities, see http://www.marginalrevolution.com/marginalrevolution/2004/01/taking_expected.html.

On the vaccine question, see Brian Zikmund-Fisher, Brianna Sarr, Angela Fagerlin, and Peter Ubel, "A Matter of Perspective: Choosing for Others Differs from Choosing for Yourself in Making Treatment Decisions," *Journal of General Internal Medicine,* June 2006, 618–622. On the economics of denial of death, see for instance Wojciech Kopczuk and Joel Slemrod, "Denial of Death and Economic Behavior," National Bureau of Economic Research working paper #11485, 2005. On how fear of death shapes our thoughts, see Sheldon Solomon, Jeff Greenberg, and Tom Pyszczynski, "Pride and Prejudice: Fear of Death and Social Behavior," *Current Directions in Psychological Science,* December 2000, 9, 6, 200–204. See also Robin Hanson's online essay "Fear of Death and Muddled Thinking—It Is So Much Worse Than You Think," available at http://hanson.gmu.edu/feardie.pdf#search=%22fear%20of%20death%20and%20muddled%20thinking%22.

For my blog post on taking care of everyone, see http://www.marginalrevolution.com/marginalrevolution/2005/11/can_we_take_car.html.

Chapter 7

On locating Afghanistan, see one survey from *National Geographic,* at http://news.nationalgeographic.com/news/2006/05/0502_060502_geography.html, accessed November 7, 2006.

On Singaporean food stalls, see for instance Ooi Giok Ling, *Future of Space: Planning, Space and the City,* Singapore: Marshall Cavendish International, 2004; Selina Ching Chan, "Consuming Food: Structuring Social Life and Creating Social Relationships," in *Past Times: A Social History of Singapore,* edited by Chan Kook Bun and Tong Chee Kiong, Singapore: Times Editions, 2000, pp. 123–135; Sylvia Tan, *Singapore Heritage Food: Yesterday's*

Recipes for Today's Cook, Singapore: Landmark Books, 2003; Chua Beng Huat, *Life Is Not Complete Without Shopping: Consumption Culture in Singapore,* Singapore: Singapore University Press, 2003.

On the Circus, Circus buffet, see Pete Earley, *Super Casino: Inside the "New" Las Vegas,* New York: Bantam Books, 2000, p. 111. On "comps," see Max Rubin, *Comp City: A Guide to Free Casino Vacations,* Las Vegas: Huntington Press, 2001, second edition, and also Michael Konik, *The Man with the $100,000 Breasts and Other Gambling Stories,* New York: Broadway Books, 1999.

Chapter 8

For one look at the trading monkeys, see "Monkey Business," Stephen Dubner and Steven Levitt, *The New York Times Magazine,* June 5, 2005, on the work of Keith Chen.

The number of eBay items is taken from an estimate by *Auction Software Review,* at http://www.auctionsoftwarereview.com/article-ebay-statistics.asp. It will likely be out of date by the time you read this.

On imaginary girlfriends, one site is http://imaginarygirlfriends.com/; for more general coverage see http://www.foxnews.com/story/0,2933,107336,00 .html. On the Japanese innovations, the arm pillow is from Kameo Corp., located in Fukuoka; see for instance http://www.msnbc.msn.com/id/6141895/. The artificial laps are made by Trane KK, here is one article: http://www .senseworldwide.com/snacks/?m=200412&paged=2.

On executives coping in prison, see "How Insider Traders Cope Inside," Christopher Bowe, *The Financial Times,* August 30, 2004, http://www.ft .com/cms/s/a30595cc-fa20-11d8-b984-00000e2511c8.html. The discussion of kidnapping draws upon, among other sources, Robert Young Pelton, *The World's Most Dangerous Places,* New York: HarperCollins, fifth edition, 2003.

On incorrectly spelled auction listings, see "In Online Auctions, Misspelling in Ads Often Spells Cash," Diana Jean Schemo, *The New York Times,* January 28, 2004, http://select.nytimes.com/search/restricted/article? res=F30811F63E5C0C7B8EDDA80894DC404482.

On buying Russian alibis for adultery, see *"Harper's* Index," February 2004. On Soundercover.com, see also "Cell Phone Software Creates Bogus Backgrounds," TheNewScientist.com News Service, March 5, 2004, http:// www.newscientist.com/article.ns?id=dn4749. On Virgin Mobile, see "Cell

Phone Hangs Up on Drunken Dialers," Iain Ferguson, November 30, 2004, http://news.com.com/2100-1039_3-5472053.html. On Mexico City prostitutes, see "Aging Prostitutes Find Champion in Mexico City Mayor, Critics Say Populist Trying to Curry Favor," by Mary Jordan, *Washington Post,* April 10, 2005, p. A20.

On www.partybuddys.com, see also Frank Owen, "An In with the In Crowd, for a Fee," *The New York Times,* January 16, 2005. On renting wedding guests, see BBC News, Saturday, September 17, 2005, at http://news.bbc.co.uk/2/hi/south_asia/4242936.stm.

The "penis restaurant" was written up in *The Telegraph,* "On the menu today: horse penis and testicles with a chilli dip," Richard Spencer, February 17, 2006. For auto-players for games, see http://gameotter.com/. The Beckham story comes from the *Daily Mirror;* here is one of many online sources: http://www.femalefirst.co.uk/celebrity/17802004.htm. On antiterrorist training, sources can be found in my blog post: http://www.marginalrevolution.com/marginalrevolution/2003/11/how_to_outfox_t.html. For protection against being buried alive, track down the sources here: http://www.marginalrevolution.com/marginalrevolution/2004/07/markets_in_ever_3.html. On testicular implants, see "Florida Canine 50,000th to Receive Silicone Testicles," pressbox.co.uk, November 12, 2000, http://www.pressbox.co.uk/Detailed/347.html; one seller is http://www.neuticles.com/index1.html. The story of Jeanette Yarborough is from *The Wall Street Journal,* December 15, 2005, p. A1.

On air rights, see for instance "Price of Air Hits Record in New York," cnn.com, November 30, 2005, http://money.cnn.com/2005/11/30/real_estate/air_rights/index.htm?cnn=yes. On paintings made by women's breasts, see an Australian news report by Sian Gard, "Replacing brushes with breasts," December 16, 2005, http://www.abc.net.au/northwestwa/stories/s1532637.htm. The discussion of synthetic games and virtual worlds is from Tim Harford, reviewing Edward Castronova's "Synthetic Worlds: The Business and Culture of On-Line Games," *The Financial Times,* January 14, 2006, p. W5.

On the work of Felix Oberholzer-Gee, see "Harvard Business School: Working Knowledge for Leaders," May 8, 2006, http://hbswk.hbs.edu/item/5319.html.

The study on how sex makes us happier, led by Daniel Kahneman, was published in the December 3, 2004, issue of *Science.* Co-authors were economist Alan B. Krueger, and psychologists David A. Schkade of the University of California, San Diego, Norbert Schwarz of the University of Michigan, and Arthur A. Stone of Stony Brook University. See also David Blanchflower and Andrew Oswald, "Money, Sex and Happiness: An Empirical Study," *Scandinavian Journal of Economics,* September 2004, 106, 3, 393–415.

For the Robert Fogel quotation, see his *The Escape from Hunger and Premature Death, 1700–2100,* Cambridge: Cambridge University Press, 2004.

Chapter 9

For which people volunteer most, see *Global Civil Society,* by Lester M. Salamon, S. Wojciech Sokolowski, and Associates, Kumarian Press, 2004. The home page of the associated project is at http://www.jhu.edu/~cnp/.

The beggars who seek to have their arms cut off is a Yahoo News story; http://news.yahoo.com/s/nm/20060801/od_nm/india_beggars_dc_1. On the time it takes to start a new business in India, see *Law, Liberty and Livelihood,* New Delhi: Academia Foundation, 2005, a new book edited by Parth Shah and Naveen Mandava of the Center for Civil Society in New Delhi.

The information on fund-raising stems from conversations from my own experience and conversations with professional fund-raisers; Kevin Gentry has been especially helpful.

On how natural disasters boost charitable giving, see Charity Navigator, http://www.charitynavigator.org/index.cfm/bay/content.view/cpid/42, data drawn from *Giving USA 2006, The Annual Report on Philanthropy.* Information on tsunami giving is from *The Chronicle of Philanthropy,* see http://philanthropy.com/free/update/2005/01/2005011901.htm.

On parachuting for charity, see C. T. Lee, P. Williams and W. A. Hadden, "Parachuting for Charity: Is It Worth the Money? A 5-year Audit of Parachute Injuries in Tayside and the Cost to the NHS," *Injury,* 30, 4, 283–287.

On the percentage of charity going to churches, see http://www.slate.com/id/2135721/, see also http://www.charitynavigator.org/index.cfm/bay/content.view/cpid/42 for a lower estimate.

For the work on John List, see, for instance, Craig Landry, Andrew Lange, John A. List, Michael K. Price, and Nicholas Rupp "Toward an Understanding of the Economics of Charity: Evidence from a Field Experiment," *Quarterly Journal of Economics,* 2006, 121, 2, 747–782, and John A.

List and David Lucking-Reiley, "The Effects of Seed Money and Refunds on Charitable Giving: Experimental Evidence from a University Capital Campaign," *Journal of Political Economy*, 2002, 110, 1, 215–233.

For information on Kristof and slave-buying, see http://kellyaward .com/mk_award_popup/kristof_n.html, and Nicholas Kristof, "Leaving the Brothel Behind," *The New York Times*, January 19, 2005, p. A19. See also "Some Simple Analytics of Slave Redemption," by Dean S. Carlan and Alan B. Krueger, at http://aida.econ.yale.edu/karlan/papers/redemption_may20-2005.doc. See also Michael Kremer and Charles Morcom, "Elephants," *American Economic Review*, March 2000, 90, 212–234, and Paul Lewis, "U.N. Criticism Angers Charities Buying Sudan Slaves' Release," *The New York Times*, March 12, 1999, p. A7.

On the pig gifts, see http://www.marginalrevolution.com/marginalrevolution/ 2003/09/you_can_always_.html, "So Scrooge Was Right After All," December 24, 2003.

On the work of Joel Waldfogel on the deadweight loss of Christmas, see his "The Deadweight Loss of Christmas," *American Economic Review*, 1993, 83, 1328–1336. On re-gifting, see for instance http://news.scotsman.com/ latest.cfm?id=1473412006 for one account of the Harris survey, based on 1,505 respondents.

On the story of Tom Locke, see http://www.marginalrevolution.com/ marginalrevolution/2006/03/an_epistolary_r.html.

On which gifts are most likely to be remembered, see the research of Leaf Van Boven; for instance, his paper with Thomas Gilovich, "To Do or to Have? That Is the Question," *Journal of Personality and Social Psychology*, 2003, 85, 1193–1202.

On Kiva, see http://www.voanews.com/specialenglish/archive/2006-08/ 2006-08-27-voa4.cfm, and here is the testimony of Cornelius: http:// matchboxcreative.com/2006/11/kivaorg-person-to-person-micro-credit.html.

Acknowledgments

My thanks go first to my family, Natasha and Yana. My friends Alex, Bryan, and Robin have provided essential input and discussions; better colleagues do not exist. Also important has been the collective wisdom provided by the readers and commenters of marginalrevolution.com, and by the blogosphere more generally. Teresa Hartnett has been a wonderful agent and a source of wise counsel throughout. Jeff Galas and Stephen Morrow have, through their advice and editing, done much to improve the manuscript and make it a real book. The Mercatus Center has supplied essential research assistance.

Index

Note: Page numbers in **bold** indicate chapters.

New from Tyler Cowen